CHILD ABUSE AND NEGLECT: AN EXAMINATION FROM THE PERSPECTIVE OF CHILD DEVELOPMENT KNOWLEDGE

JEANNE M. GIOVANNONI, JONATHON CONKLIN, AND PATTI IIYAMA

San Francisco, California
1978

PUBLISHED BY

R & E RESEARCH ASSOCIATES, INC.
936 INDUSTRIAL AVENUE
PALO ALTO, CALIFORNIA 94303

PUBLISHERS

ROBERT D. REED AND ADAM S. ETEROVICH

Library of Congress Card Catalog Number
77-90387

I.S.B.N.
0-88247-514-2

This work was supported through Grant #86-P-80086/9 from Social and Rehabilitation Services, Office of Research and Demonstration, U. S. Department of Health, Education and Welfare.

TABLE OF CONTENTS

CHAPTER 1

INTRODUCTION

The problems of child abuse and neglect have gained national attention in recent years. This growth in national interest has not solved the controversy as to what kinds of specific actions by caretakers should be considered abusive or neglectful, although in the extremes there appears to be a consensus. Most child development experts agree that if a child is beaten until a bone is broken, that child is being abused. They also agree that a child willfully starved to death is one who was neglected. As we move away from such extremes, however, the consensus is replaced by controversy. This is particularly true of actions that might be considered neglectful -- actions that are not physically damaging to children, but are psychologically or emotionally harmful.

Research interests in the field of child abuse and neglect have tended to focus on the less extreme conditions, but we have tried to include work from all parts of the spectrum. Our literature review was restricted to studies that examined variables specifically related to caretaking behavior. For example, although social class is considered an important variable in child development, if a study did not relate that variable to caretaking behavior and its effect on the child, it was not included. In limiting our selection of studies to empirical research, neither case studies that drew conclusions only from clinical speculation, nor theoretical studies that were not based on some empirical work were included.

Our information was obtained from reviewing the written research on children and from consulting experts in child-related research. Our report presents the results of both these efforts. Hopefully, this will serve as a beginning compendium of facts for resolving some of the controversy. We have tried to establish a basis for determining which actions or inactions on the part of caretakers should be considered abusive or neglectful to children and are therefore reasonably certain to cause harm or impair development.

The material has been organized into three categories -- physical, mental, and social-emotional development. In reality, these aspects of development are interdependent, but these divisions serve as a framework for studying the effects of dependent variables on child development. In fact, the same study can appear in different sections due to the interlocking of variables under investigation.

Our method for locating the research was to undertake a bibliographic search utilizing the MEDLINE computerized bibliography and the Educational Resources Information Center (ERIC) and Child Development Abstracts. The MEDLINE file searches 2,300 journals and ERIC has a data base of 800 journals. On the basis of the vocabulary utilized for the search in MEDLINE, 641 titles were received (see Appendix I). The ERIC search presented a substantial printout of annotated references, of which the vast majority were general reviews or non-empirical studies that did not meet the specific requirements of this review. The Child Development Abstracts were reviewed from 1960 through 1975 and, on the basis of title and content, articles were selected and screened for final review.

We are grateful to the consultants who gave such deep and thoughtful consideration to the questions that we posed and who in turn raised equally thoughtful questions about our pursuit. Dr. Robert Brockman conducted the interviews with them and Ms. Margaret Kisliuk typed the manuscript.

CHAPTER 2

PROBLEMS OF DEFINITION OF "ABUSE" AND "NEGLECT"

Definitional Issues in "Abuse" and "Neglect"

Uniform definitions of abuse and neglect do not exist. But the issues in the problem transcend mere ambiguity of words and rest upon deeper ambiguities in the concepts themselves. We have identified at least four conceptual problem areas: (1) the multiplicity of uses of the terms, not all of which are compatible, (2) the lack of specificity of referents to the ideas expressed in the abstract definitions, (3) the parameters, and the nature of the parameters, of what is encompassed by the terms, and (4) the ambiguity of the components of the terms.

"Abuse" and "neglect" are terms that are part of at least four different vocabularies: they are legal terms, medical terms, social work terms, and lay terms. At least part of the ambiguity in meaning stems from this multiplicity of usage for different purposes. As legal, especially legislative terms, the principal purpose of the words is to serve as guidelines for judicial action. Somehow, the notion of a continuum from acceptable to unacceptable parenting is always implied, with a point at which legal action can be justified. Legal definitions must be sufficiently clear to delineate acts encompassed by the term from other, possibly overlapping, ones and to offer at least a guideline as to the threshold for action. Hence, although the terms are exceedingly vague, the language in laws regarding abuse and neglect identifies which perpetrators are and are not included and also specifies some degree on a continuum, e.g., "severe" physical injury or "conditions such that the child is in danger."

As medical and social work terms, the idea of degree or continuum seems to be of less paramount importance. For both social work and medicine, the words abuse and neglect are primarily diagnostic categories. Practitioners tend to treat categories wholistically and to refine the meanings by establishing subcategories and new categories. To a certain extent in both professions the term connotes a condition and an etiology, a treatment or corrective modality. In medicine, to avoid ambiguity "non-accidental trauma" substitutes for abuse and there is at least one specifiable subcategory of "neglect" -- "failure to thrive."

Since social work is similar to law in its investigatory functions, it also takes into account the matter of degree with respect to actionable behavior. But the social work literature on the subject has been preoccupied with establishing subcategories, e.g., physical versus emotional abuse or neglect, sexual abuse, and others. In the field of social work, the terms "abuse" and "neglect" and their subcategories serve as diagnostic categories and in addition define arenas of work that require particular kinds of skills and knowledge of specialized practitioners. The wholistic interpretation of abuse and neglect, however, still dominates in order to facilitate communication within the profession. In a sense, as with any professional language, the words take on a life and a meaning of their own and the fitting of individual cases into appropriate categories, or diagnoses, becomes a basis for action.

"Abuse" and "neglect" as lay terms are widely used and they are as likely to appear in Good Housekeeping or the "Sunday supplement" as they are in professional journals. The average person is expected to understand the terms in at least a quasi-professional sense and in fact many exercise their own initiative by categorizing actions as "neglectful" or "abusive" when they report or make complaints to agencies. Although a great deal is not known about the lay conceptualization of abuse and neglect, it seems likely that lay persons treat the concepts in a wholistic manner, rather than as degrees along a continuum.

The confusing nature of the concepts as matters of degree or as wholistic discrete entities makes it difficult to establish the parameters of what is subsumed under the categories of "abuse" and "neglect." Another area of ambiguity is whether the concepts refer to the condition of a child or to the factors that contributed to or produced that condition. Are actions abusive or neglectful, regardless of the impact or harm to the child? Or, conversely, should actions that harm the child be excluded because of other factors in the situation or in the person responsible (e.g., ignorance, willfulness, or mitigating circumstances)? Are "abuse" and "neglect" limited to certain harmful conditions in children that are the result of still other specifiable, but limited, conditions? While the lack of precision is understandable, the implications of the imprecision are far-reaching.

Implications of the Lack of Conceptual Clarity and Definitional Precision

The lack of a clear-cut definition and conceptual clarity has series implications at three levels of operation in the areas of neglect and abuse. These three areas are: (1) research, (2) social practice, and (3) policy formulation and management.

The implications for research are clear. If it is not possible to specify what is meant in operational terms by abuse and neglect, how does one specify what is being studied? How are populations to be selected and how are crucial variables to be measured? Many have commented on this deficiency in the research that does exist, especially in the area of neglect. In an effort to overcome the deficiency, some have advocated the establishment of measures independent of the identification process by official agencies. (For the most part, definitions rest on designations by official agencies.) Such solutions, however, are problematic in that it is not known whether populations selected through these independent measures are equivalent to those being managed by the official agencies. Hence, applicability to practice of findings from such research has been questioned. Alternatively, the field is stymied with an operational definition that amounts to little more than the official designation of "neglect."

In understanding what is encompassed by the terms in practice and policy, two matters are of recurrent concern. The first involves the inseparable issues of parental rights and management of abuse and neglect. In the context of American society, legal parents have the legal right to refuse governmental intervention into matters of childrearing -- within certain boundaries and limits. Insofar as abuse or neglect become the substantive reasons for making the judgment that such boundaries and limits have been exceeded and hence the parents' legal right to refuse intrusion may be overridden, there is a constant demand upon those who must make the judgments to set the parameters of what does and does not constitute abuse and neglect. The definitional imprecision of the concepts of abuse and neglect inevitably hampers the rationality of the decisions. Decisions of resource allocation are as integral to the work of the direct practitioner as they are to those at the policy, legislative, and administrative levels. Assuming that in most American economic matters we always operate from a basis of scarcity, the individual practitioner must always decide which families and which children will or will not receive their services.

Similarly, at the policy and administrative levels, decisions must be made as to how much and what kinds of resources are worth allocating. Such decisions involve all levels of government. While at the federal level there may be some uniformity of criteria, at the state and local level there is an enormous range in the amounts allocated to the management of neglect and abuse. Such variation partly reflects the looseness of definition of the terms; in countries and states with scarcer resources, and hence greater competition in allocation, the bounda-

5

ries of what constitutes abuse and neglect may well be narrowed, thereby keeping
the potential recipient population at a minimum.

Thus, whether the concepts of "neglect" and "abuse" are treated in policy
wholistically or as matters of degree along a continuum, a rationale must be developed for determining what is abuse or neglect, or what is of sufficient concern to intervene into families' lives or to allocate resources for such intervention.

"Adequate" - "Optimal" - "Minimal"

Before beginning our analysis, it is important to explain how we have tried
to handle two conceptual dilemmas that seem inevitable in our inquiry. The first
problem is the semantic trap of demarcating the degrees of "harm" or distinguishing between harmful and not harmful by simply substituting other words, such as
"adequate" or "minimal," that still beg the same questions. The use of "optimal," "adequate," and "harmful" and the potential for delineating these along
any kind of continuum underscore the ways in which "abuse" and "neglect" are
used and the difficulty in assessing harm from the accumulated knowledge of
child development research.

As noted at the outset, "abuse" and "neglect" are legal and social work
terms, for which, within given parameters, a course of action is prescribed. In
legal terms, if a child is being abused, neglected or harmed in any way, this
implies a rationale for interfering with parental rights. In social work terms
this implies the allocation of services. And so, in both the legal and social
work sense, the question becomes: is the child being harmed enough to warrant
intervention and to be allocated services? In the area of cognitive stimulation,
what is enough harm -- demonstrable mental retardation? Six months behind the
norm in reading ability? A seven-point difference on an I.Q. test? Child development research may be able to give definitive answers to the outcomes of various actions for children, but it cannot answer these kinds of questions, which
are issues involving major societal values.

The ideas of "adequate" and "optimal" development also reflect another aspect of child development research on the question of harm. While there is a
vast body of child development research, much of it is geared toward answering
questions about optimal development; the question posed is really "what is good
for children," not "what harms them." There is probably a practical reason for
this: the most carefully designed research, especially that using experimental
design, is not likely to have as a dependent variable something that is grossly

harmful to children. Indeed, grossly harmed children are not likely to be included in research that is directed toward development in the normal range. Such
children, when studied, are more likely to be studied outside the laboratory
with ex post facto designs.

The discussion of optimate environments for stimulation ultimately concerns
the notion of total environment and the child, not solely the parent and the
child. This has real implications for the definition of neglect, whether it is
defined from the standpoint of environmental impact on the child or only from
that of the parents' behavior. Conceivably, children can be in total environments where they receive adequate stimulation, such as day nurseries, while
their parents are unable to provide such stimulation. From the standpoint of
children, their need for stimulation is not being neglected, although in fact
the parents may be behaving in a neglectful way. Thus, "neglect" or "harm" cannot be defined out of the context of the total environment.

Physical/Emotional Dichotomy

The problem of separating out the physical, cognitive, and emotional domains
is actually one that pervades our entire line of inquiry. It, of course, reflects similar dilemmas in the present four-fold categorization of physical neglect and abuse and emotional neglect and abuse. We have found it useful to
separate the distinctions made for purposes of analysis of the various areas of
children's experiences and the social value attached to each area of life. By
"social value" we simply mean that there seems to exist a hierarchy of harms;
"physical" harm is worse or of more urgent concern that "emotional" and "cognitive" damage is probably also considered to be worse than "emotional." Hence,
there is the legal notion of intervention only "in case of immediate physical
danger," which is currently under attack by those who argue that "emotional"
damage is at least as "bad" or even "worse" than physical damage. Insofar as
possible, we have tried to avoid this kind of distinction.

We have, however, given considerable stress to the analytic distinctions
and the consequences for interpreting research findings when the variables studied are so categorized. Indeed, the interaction of "physical," "cognitive," and
"emotional" variables is so complex as to render meaningless the practical distinctions between physical and emotional neglect. For example, the physical
condition of malnourishment in a child may be the result of a complex interplay
of factors in the environment, none of which might be considered physical, but
which would be judged to be affective or emotional. Similarly, some conditions

7

of undernutrition might be of concern not because they are physically disabling or life threatening, but rather because the condition might impair the child's cognitive development. It is important to clarify these matters at the outset lest some of the research issues and findings discussed be misinterpreted.

There is already some evidence of this kind of misinterpretation in the literature on child neglect. In their understandably zealous efforts to obtain support for the neglected child equal to that of the physically abused child, some advocates have sought to establish the far-reaching physical effects of neglect. One example is the common reference to children who died during World War II, presumably as a result of not having any mothering person near them. Such references all too quickly seem to equate or even to supplant for the concept of "maternal deprivation" meaning no mothering person, a meaning that implies a deficiency in mothering by a mother who, although she may be deficient, is there. Such blurring of meaning is a misuse of research findings that, rather than aiding in understanding "neglect," can only serve to further our confusion.

The original question that we posed -- "What is harmful to children?" -- is based on a model that seems to exemplify the present pursuit of knowledge on child neglect and abuse. From a legal standpoint, efforts are made to demonstrate that children are being harmed as a result of certain caretaker behaviors. From an interventive standpoint, efforts are made to understand and correct the causes of the errant caretakers' behavior. A kind of two-stage etiologic process is involved, which can be diagrammatically presented as follows:

Etiology of Caretaker Behavior	Etiology of Harm to Child, Caretaker Behavior	Harmful Effect on Child
e.g., maternal psycho-pathology due to early life experience	e.g., maternal deprivation, emotional neglect	e.g., malnutrition, failure-to-thrive

The inadequacy of this model and its oversimplication of the problem were brought out repeatedly in our investigation. A major facet of this oversimplication is the failure of such a model to account for what children bring to situations potentially harmful to them. At a very basic level, a designation of harm cannot be made without consideration of factors resident in children.

CHAPTER 3

WHAT THE CHILD BRINGS TO THE SITUATION

This theme in our consultants' discussions regarding both general and specific harms to children might be termed differential vulnerability among children due to their own characteristics. In other words, some children will be harmed by some conditions while others will not be affected. Our consultants referred to innate individual differences in response to a number of our questions, particularly those concerning the reversibility of damages, as well as the initial infliction of harm. With respect to innate differences among infants, several important perspectives emerged: (1) the impact of innate qualities on children's later development, (2) the impact of these qualities on mothers' response to their babies, and (3) the quality of mother-child interaction.

Children's Endowment and Their Development

Both Dr. Anneliese F. Korner, whose work as been with normal infants, and Dr. Donald J. Cohen, who deals with atypical children, cited the importance of congenital or inherent determinants in children's development. The significance of this perspective is not limited to ideas about what is or is not neglectful or abusive behavior. These comments also have direct relevance to research interpretation in the etiology of neglect and abuse, particularly that focusing exclusively on maternal psychopathology and deriving from earlier work that was intended to explain the pathology of mothers whose maternal behavior was thought to produce mental illness in their children. Insofar as a biologic or congenital component is likely to be a factor in the development of such illness, those in the field of child neglect would do well to treat with caution findings that ascribe all blame to maternal pathology.

Dr. Korner cited the "organismic characteristics of a given child" as a very important intervening variable in predicting consequences of child care for children. This conceptualization of organismic characteristics as intervening variables rather than as sole determinants of development is useful in determining the context for thinking about harm to children and in eliminating an either/or stance with regard to determinants of children's development. This is particularly true with reference to behavioral and affective development. The importance of inherent qualities in the situation of the autistic child was emphasized by Dr. Cohen:

> There is a whole spectrum of atypicality, because there are some children who are vulnerable and on the border between being able to be adaptive and non-adaptive, but who in very stressful environments don't make it. And there are other children who, regardless of what kind of family they go into, are really going to be autistic.

He noted that the parents of autistic children actually had been abused by professionals for many years, because the professionals themselves were confounded by the autism and therefore blamed the parents. That situation is similar to psychosocial dwarfism today where the imputation of parental responsibility is made almost by default. Because the child has not thrived while living with the parents, but seems to thrive after being separated from the parents, the parents are then considered to be the noxious agents. What seems apparent is that the thinking to date is based on an association between the child's thriving and the environment in which the child lives. But the explanation of that association, the drawing of an etiologic link, is not yet established.

This dilemma is similar to the debate on the importance of congenital factors in understanding children's functioning, especially with respect to behavior. Some people are more prone to treat what the children bring to the world and what goes on in their central nervous systems as independent variables, while others see congenital factors as dependent variables. A more complex interpretation of the relationship between the child and the environment centers on the question of the extent to which congenital factors create or shape the child's environment. There is the possibility that congenital factors might allow for more adventuresome behavior in some children which in turn evokes more stimulation from the environment.

The literature on child neglect has paid little attention to congenital issues. We are not drawing any conclusions about the influence of congenital factors on problems endemic to neglected children, but rather consider the issue of children's endowments as an excellent illustration of the complexities and pitfalls in defining neglect. This is particularly true in the more profound manifestations of dysfunction in children where there is no question that a child is afflicted with a very serious, harmful condition, but where the issue is whether the parents or caretakers are responsible for that condition.

Mother-Child Interaction

The contribution of a child's endowment to "creating an environment" is integrally related to problems in mother-child interaction. Current research on mother-child interaction focuses on infant temperament as the independent variable; researchers are looking at what the infant brings to the interaction and how the infant elicits certain kinds of behavior from the mother. For example, a highly active infant may have a dissonant interaction with a mother who is more restrained and inhibited in her activity. Such dissonant interactions can then lead to problems between the two that might be classified as "neglectful" or even "abusive." One would not expect, however, to find any kind of invariant relationship between particular sets of maternal personality characteristics and the quality of interaction with infants. Perhaps the problem must be reconceptualized as resulting not from noxious mothers, but rather from noxious pairings, or at least of pairings with the potential for harmful effects on the child's development.

These observations on mother-infant interaction are similar to those on older children. Dr. Ernesto Pollitt found no clear-cut psychopathological signs to distinguish the mothers of growth-retarded children. He noted that this was contrary to the common assumption about failure-to-thrive, that the character and personality of the mother are considered to be contributing factors to the disorder. Mothers of the index children had a greater incidence of traumatic childhood experiences and has had multiple caretakers as children themselves. His interpretation of these data is that mothers of growth-retarded children do not necessarily demonstrate any clear-cut psychopathological signs. Rather, the child might bring to the relationship some attributes that are idiosyncratic and that may demand a caretaker who is more dedicated than usual. If the mother has had a traumatic life, problems in caretaking are apt to develop, despite the absence of any specifiable character disorder.

A large gap also exists in this research on mother-child interaction: the almost total absence of research including fathers. Some such research is now in process, although there is great difficulty in conceptualizing a triadic relationship, as opposed to the more easily grouped diadic one. This difficulty, rather than any known unimportance of fathers, underlies this gap in the research.

Impact of Parental Ignorance of Individual Differences

Thus far we have considered particular child-centered factors that either might interact with the children's environment in ways potentially harmful to them or that might mitigate the effects of otherwise harmful conditions. There is another way in which individual differences among children might precipitate either actual harm or less than optimal caretaking: many parents are ignorant of the differences that exist among infants and children and of the variety of behavior required to respond to these differences.

As Dr. Donald Cohen noted,

> parents often do not know what infants are really like and what they really need. I would think that most neglected children are not neglected because of the bad motivations of their parents. I think that a lack of understanding can lead to kinds of interactions that might become destructive. For example, if people who are particularly sensitive to babies' crying and fussing do not have any understanding of the reasons for this crying, they can become more and more irritated by the babies and can set up a pattern of harsh, neglectful behavior.

Hence, the widespread lack of understanding of individual differences among infants and children must be considered a potentially hazardous condition for children.

Children's Perceptions and Harm

Before leaving this section on child-centered factors that might contribute to harmful situations for children, another level of child-oriented factors must be considered: children's perceptions of their treatment. These perceptions might be the key ingredient in whether or not a child is damaged in the total context of a situation or relationship. Of particular importance is the view that such perceptions are engendered as much by the culture in which children live as by their familial environment. For older children, the extrafamilial environment probably is an even stronger determinant of such perceptions.

This perceptual context is important in determining the emotional impact of physical punishment as well as in trying to delineate the fine line between pathological and non-pathological physical punishment. Some children perceive physical punishment as an indication of caring, particularly in families where a great deal of physical contact of an affectionate nature is characteristic. Such physical punishment is viewed as a way of socializing a child, as opposed to punishment that is violence with the intent to hurt the child.

Cultural differences are crucial to understanding what might not be considered nurturant parental behavior and possibly wrongly considered as "neglectful" by outsiders when, in fact, children are being nurtured in a way unfamiliar to the observer. As Dr. Jerome Kagan stated,

> In each culture there are signs by which you know you are loved. In ours it's physical affection, but that's not true all over the world. If a child is not given physical affection, he begins to wonder because that's what he sees

on television, that's what the books say; you kiss and hug
the people you love. Children in Norway, where there's not
a lot of kissing and hugging, wouldn't begin to feel that
they were rejected. The ingredients that go into the perception of being loved, of being valued, are relative and
they are not in a specified act by a parent. A white Ap-
palachian mother does not communicate her love the way a
Jewish Los Angeles mother does; yet the children of both
feel valued.

This view then adds to factors resident in the child, cultural and sub-
cultural influences on children's expectations and perceptions that can set the
conditions under which a given parental act or behavior might or might not be
harmful. Consensus does not exist as to the relative strength of the child's
contribution and there is no comparable certainty about the specific infant characteristics that might clash with particular maternal personality traits. But
there is a consensus on the importance of what children bring to situations of
potential harm.

Many investigators, however, have not incorporated this important perspective into their studies. Understanding these limitations, we will look now at
the research pertinent to the field of child abuse and neglect. Much of the research has been concentrated on the factors affecting physical development of
the child, since they are more easily quantifiable than other factors.

CHAPTER 4

PHYSICAL DEVELOPMENT

Low Birth Weight

Among the potential risks to children's development, low birth weight is perhaps the earliest visible sign that physical development of an infant is subnormal. Hospitals usually treat low birth weight infants as populations "at risk," placing them in a separate ward ("premature" unit) and giving them special care. Low birth weight is generally recognized as a risk not only in terms of immediate survival but also in terms of future problems. Our discussion will consider those areas of later risk and survey those factors before and during pregnancy that are found to be significantly associated with the occurrence of low birth weight. As an accompanying problem of low birth weight, low gestational age is also viewed as an early but separate risk and is reviewed in this section.

Although the term "prematurity" is often used interchangeably with the concept of low birth weight, this discussion makes a distinction between the concepts of low birth weight and low gestational age. The most common conception of low birth weight is that the infant, born before the full term of gestation, has been deprived of a certain amount of fetal growth before birth. In other cases, however, the birth weight is lower than would be expected for a particular gestational age. These infants with "low birth weight for gestational age" are usually small because of inadequate intrauterine growth.

Prenatal Correlates of Low Birth Weight

Diverse factors may lead to low birth weight including the following: maternal disease, poor maternal diet, small placentas, infection, and genetic abnormalities (Chase, 1973). Because maternal diet is most amenable to outside influence, it is the factor that may be most relevant to a discussion of child neglect. Inadequacy of maternal diet may result in infants who have not thrived nutritionally in utero and are thus low in birth weight for gestational age.

Evidence given and cited by several theorists (Chase, 1973; Naeye et al., 1973; Metcoff et al., 1971; Miller and Hassanein, 1973) indicates that this hypothesis may be valid. Metcoff et al. (1971) compared 70 mother-infant pairs,

14

of which 29 infants were of normal birth weight, 26 infants were of low birth weight but of appropriate weight for gestational age, and 15 infants were of low birth weight that was more than two standard deviations below the birth weight expected for their gestational ages. Metabolic similarities were noted between the leukocytes of intrauterine growth-retarded infants and protein-calorie malnourished infants. These findings were interpreted as supporting the thesis that intrauterine growth retardation primarily reflects intrauterine undernutrition. The investigators concluded that intrauterine undernutrition can interfere with the biological development of the fetus at various times during gestation and can lead to poor cell function. Furthermore, maternal malnutrition might subtly influence fetal development without evidence of overt clinical malnutrition in the mother. It was suggested that the diagnosis of fetal undernutrition may be possible from a biomolecular analysis of maternal leukocytes early in pregnancy and before delivery.

Naeye, Blanc, and Paul (1973) examined 467 autopsy protocols of stillborn and newborn infants whose gestational ages ranged from 18 to 44 weeks. They correlated fetal body, organ, and cellular growth with the mothers' prepregnancy, mid- and late gestational nutritional status. Their results showed that maternal pregravid body weight as well as weight gain during gestation did show such a relationship. Maternal prepregnancy weight and very high or very low gestational weight gain had only a small effect on the body and organ measurements of neonates who were born before 33 weeks of gestation, but the effects of these maternal weight extremes were significant in late gestation. In all nutritional categories, newborn body and organ growth was significantly smaller for mothers who had been placed on a specific low-calorie diet than for mothers who had followed general dietary advice.

Unlike postnatal undernutrition, the problem of intrauterine undernutrition is difficult to diagnose. The effects must usually be inferred from the infant's status at birth, rather than observed in utero. It is often impossible to ascertain the fetus's ongoing nutritional needs except to assess the average minimal requirements in relation to the mother's current diet. Thus, unlike postnatal undernutrition, a mother is unlikely to know that she has neglected to provide adequately for her infant's intrauterine nutritional needs until well after the effects of such neglect have taken place. For this reason, intrauterine undernutrition may constitute a more serious problem than is generally recognized by professionals and the public.

A number of other factors that might be associated with fetal undernutrition have also been examined. Miller and Hassanein (1973) compared 33 full-term infants whose ratios of birth weight to body length were below the third percentile with a control group of 132 full-term infants of normal birth weight-length ratios on the incidence of selected maternal factors. Their results showed that maternal factors significantly associated with severe fetal undernutrition included poor maternal weight gain during pregnancy preeclampsia, the occurrence of major chronic illness, the absence of prenatal clinical visits, unmarried status, and obesity. On the other hand, maternal factors significantly associated with the birth of well-nourished infants included a mean weight gain of one pound or more per week in the last two trimesters of pregnancy and extensive prenatal clinic visits. Given the array of variables studied, it is quite possible that unstudied variables may account for two or more of these correlates (e.g., is there a common variable that underlies the association between prenatal clinic visits and maternal undernutrition?).

Ferreira (1965) presented a very comprehensive review of a large number of studies dealing with the effects of prenatal environmental factors on the fetus and concluded that low birth weight can be prompted by adverse maternal emotional conflicts. In addition, he cited evidence that excessive maternal weight before pregnancy and maternal smoking during pregnancy are both associated with greater incidence of low birth weight. As with most of the issues in the general field, however, contrary evidence exists that maternal emotional conflict does not cause low birth weight. Ottinger and Simmons (1964) compared 19 neonates and their mothers of whom ten had scored high on the IPAT Anxiety Scale during pregnancy and nine had scored low. Their results showed that the two groups of high and low maternal anxiety did not result in differing infant birth weight.

In a retrospective study of the fetal complications of maternal heroin addiction as evidenced by the neonates of 82 heroin-addicted mothers, Naeye et al. (1973) found that low birth weight was associated with acute infection and deficient organ cellularity brought on by fetal exposure to heroin, as well as with maternal undernutrition. Sussman (1963) investigated the effects of narcotic and methamphetamine use during pregnancy by 19 addicted mothers on their neonates and found that more than half of the infants were of low birth weights. These studies seem to indicate that maternal use of certain drugs during pregnancy adversely affects fetal development.

Noxious Correlates of Fetal Undernutrition

The possibility that low birth weight might have a permanent retarding

effect on mental development or capacity has been suggested by a number of studies. Willerman and Churchill (1967) administered the WISC to 27 sets of identical twins and found that within sets the twin with the lower birth weight had
lower verbal and performance IQ scores than the heavier twin sibling. This
birth weight-IQ relationship was demonstrated in a group of white middle-class
twins as well as in a racially mixed lower-SES group selected on the basis of
their poor school performance. In a longitudinal study on the relationship between low birth weight and later intellectual and psychological functioning, 442
low birth weight children (less than 2,5000 gm.) were examined at six to seven
years of age (Wiener et al., 1965) and 417 of those children were reexamined at
eight to ten years of age (Wiener, 1970) on a number of tests of psychological
and intellectually impaired, even with race, maternal attitudes and practices,
and social class factors simultaneously controlled. The degree of impairment
was significant and appeared to increase with decreasing birth weight.

Chase (1973) in a review of a number of animal and human studies raised
the possibility of reversing the effects of low birth weight. He cited evidence
that intrauterine undernutrition is related to significant reductions in brain
weight, brain cellularity, and the presence of brain myelin lipids. He also
pointed out, however, that, inasmuch as major portions of brain development occur in postnatal life, the effects of intrauterine undernutrition on such development may be reversible given good postnatal nutritional care.

Several investigators have identified other areas of risk that may be associated with low birth weight. De Hirsch, Jansky, and Langford (1966) longitudinally compared 53 children of birth weights less than 2,500 gm. with 53 children of normal birth weights on tests of motor ability, perception, language and
reading ability, and investment of effort. All of the children chosen were of
normal intelligence, but the low birth weight children did less well than did
maturely born peers on the battery of tests administered at kindergarten age.
Although there seemed to be a trend in several cases toward improvement, significant lags persisted well into the eighth year of life. The investigators noted
that, perhaps as a result of physiological deficits, the low birth weight children were less able to tolerate stress and continued to exhibit the normal stages
of infantile dependency at a considerably later age than did the normal birth
weight children. Williams and Scarr (1971) investigated the functioning levels
of low birth weight children and the effects of short-term intervention. They
suggested that the combination of environmental and physiological handicaps present in many low birth weight children may severely limit both sensory input and

17

the ability to process sensory input. In a long-term follow-up study of 91 ten-year-old children who had birth weights of less than 1,500 gm., Lubchenco et al. (1972) administered complete medical, neurologic, ophthalmologic, and psychometric examinations and found a high overall incidence (50 percent) of handicaps (e.g., spastic diplegia, learning problems, retrolental fibroplasia). The highest incidence of handicaps occurred in the smallest infants of shortest gestational age and the lowest incidence occurred in the largest infants with a weight above 1,450 gm. and 33 weeks gestation.

A number of studies have also been conducted on the relationship between low birth weight and mental health. Katz and Taylor (1967) compared the birth records of 573 mentally retarded children with those of a population of normal children. A significantly greater number of retarded children than normal children (25 percent vs. 5 percent) had birth weights of less than 2,500 gm. Matheny and Brown (1971) longitudinally studied behavioral differences related to differences in birth weight between 49 sets of twins, which suggest prenatal factors as a cause. Their results showed that twins who were small for gestational age tended to exhibit more "problem" behaviors, such as irritability, feeding problems, and sleeping problems, and were relatively less proficient on aspects of cognitive behaviors, such as attention span, vocalization, and adaptability, than their twin siblings of appropriate weight for gestational age.

In a retrospective study of 51 cases of abused children seen over a period of nine years at the Montreal Children's Hospital, Klein and Stern (1971) found a significantly higher incidence of low birth weight (less than 2,500 gm.) than was expected on the basis of Quebec perinatal figures: 23.5 percent of the abused children had a low birth weight, compared to seven percent of the children born in Quebec. They concluded that, in cases of low birth weight, the enforced separation commonly practiced in premature units contributes to abnormal maternal-child relationships, including rejection, neglect, and, finally, abuse. It must be noted, of course, that while this is a higher incidence of low birth weight than the norm, it could hardly be described as characteristic of the abused group since 76.5 percent of them had not experienced low birth weight.

Other investigators have examined the possibility of a relationship between socioeconomic conditions and low birth weight. On the basis of their comprehensive follow-up study of 135 low birth weight children and 92 control children when the children were approximately eight to ten years old, Robinson and Robinson (1965) noted that low birth weight is associated with poor socioeconomic status; with maternal age, health, and medical care; and with a number of complications of pregnancy that may help to bring about low birth weight or that may be caused by the same set of circumstances as low birth weight. Klein and Stern (1971) found a higher than normal percentage of low birth weight children later identified as cases of child abuse and cited existing evidence that such factors as poverty, deprivation, social class, and alcoholism tend to be associated with low birth weight. In particular, they pointed to an increased incidence of low birth weight infants among women from deprived socioeconomic backgrounds where prenatal care is either not available or underutilized.

Evidence against the separability of the long-term effects of low birth weight and the milieu in which the child is reared has been found by Robinson and Robinson (1965) in a comprehensive follow-up study of eight to ten-year-old children, of whom 92 had weighed more than 2,500 gm. at birth, 102 had birth weights between 1,501 and 2,500 gm., and 33 had weighed 1,500 gm. or less. Their results failed to suggest that the two groups of low birth weight children fared any less well (on a number of variables including IQ) than might have been expected from a knowledge of their social class backgrounds. Children of low birth weight, however, did on the average remain physically smaller than did children whose weight at birth was normal.

Summary

In summary, it appears that low birth weight and low gestational age are both related to general areas of later risk. Ideally, both birth weight and gestational age should be taken into account when investigating the developmental effects of premature birth and other birth-condition problems. Most of the research, however, has been concerned with the effects of low birth weight alone or has failed to make the distinction between birth weights that are small and those that are appropriate for gestational age. Although there have been numerous studies on the topic, there appears to be relatively little agreement as to whether low birth weight in and of itself carries any particular risk to the child. The ambiguity of the results of studies of the subsequent effects of low birth weight on children is apparent.

Significant associations have been found between low birth weight/low gestational age and such later problems as: intellectual and psychological impairment, perceptual problems, medical, neurological, and learning handicaps, behavioral problems, physical growth impairment, mental retardation, and even child abuse. Controversy exists, however, as to the strength of environmental factors during development upon low birth weight. A number of maternal and environmental factors have also been indicated as possible precursors to low birth weight, including: intrauterine undernutrition, complications in pregnancy, poor maternal health, lack of medical care, maternal emotional problems during pregnancy, and smoking or drug addiction during pregnancy. The factor perhaps most significantly associated with low birth weight and some of its later risks is that of low socioeconomic status, for most of the factors mentioned above occur more often among poor and poverty-stricken mothers. Less is known about specific poverty-induced conditions that might account for the strength of this association, such as a higher incidence of younger age mothers, the specifics of their nutritional states, and their greater vulnerability to disease. Until refinements in measuring the specific effects of poverty are realized, little in specific areas of corrective interventions is likely to be developed.

Although these studies do point out some possible areas of risk that may be related to low birth weight or to low gestational age, it must be emphasized that the data remain at a correlational level and untangling the causal chains remains a difficult task. Because it is unlikely that independent variables such as low birth weight will ever be manipulated in human subjects, such questions of causality will probably continue to be unanswered. But the significant associations evidenced between low birth weight and subsequent factors of risk do give reason for concern, for if the factors predisposing to the incidence of low birth weight are identifiable and therefore controllable, then perhaps some of the later risks can also be minimized. Even though this is an issue that seems to invite research, there are few studies concerned with the identification of factors that may predispose to low birth weight. The long-range effects of low birth weight on development and the relative contribution of postnatal developmental environmental factors remain clouded and confused. In view of these limitations, low birth weight is perhaps best considered as an index measure, although it is not certain precisely what low birth weight indicates.

Early Growth Failure

Perhaps no other category of risk under the general rubric of physical development has been so visible and attracted so much public attention as that of early growth failure. Mere mention of the word "neglect" commonly evokes images of the starving or stunted child living in poverty. Although it seems logical to relate growth failure primarily to neglect, several studies identify it as a common feature in cases of child abuse, indicating that the conceptual distinction between abuse and neglect may be hazy. Krieger (1974) studied ten cases of "psychosocial deprivation dwarfism" at the Children's Hospital in Michigan and found that, although all of the children had been of normal birth and birth weights, nine of them had manifested growth failure before the age of two. Direct and indirect evidence suggested that their food had been intentionally and persistently restricted at home. Krieger proposed that such food restriction is actually a form of child abuse and results from an intense maternal rejection of the child. He further postulated that such rejection is often highly related to the mother's past: to being rejected herself or constantly belittled as a child.

In a longitudinal study, Elmer and Gregg (1967) re-evaluated 20 children five years after they had been treated as cases of child abuse at the Children's Hospital in Pittsburgh. A review of hospital records showed that many of the children had been below the third percentile in physical growth for their age at the time of hospital treatment. That is, early growth failure was found to be a common developmental characteristic of many of the cases of abuse. Additional results of the study showed that all seven of the children who were living in substitute homes or in institutions had fully recovered physically, whereas those who were still living in their original homes either remained below normal or had fallen below the third percentile in physical growth.

In the existing literature, growth failure is most often equated with the concept of deprivation. The basic concept is that growth retardation results from the lack of some factor that is essential to proper growth. Based upon review of a number of studies, two general categories of deprivation emerge: environmental and psychosocial. Environmental deprivation refers primarily to the unavailability or lack of intake of nutritional foodstuffs that are essential for normal growth. Psychosocial deprivation, often called "emotional" or "maternal deprivation," refers to a lack of proper psychological or social nurturance and most often is thought to reflect some kind of disorder in the maternal-child interaction. Although psychosocial deprivation may result in environmental deprivation (as in the case of feeding-behavior disturbances), it often results in growth failure despite adequate nutritional intake (as in the case of non-organic "failure-to-thrive"). Whatever the interaction, both categories of deprivation may result in early growth failure.

Before proceeding with this investigation, two general guidelines must be clarified. First, growth retardation may be caused by organic disease or congenital metabolic problems. The direct relevance of these issues to the general topic of child abuse and neglect, however, is minimal and they are therefore excluded from this discussion. Secondly, the definition of growth failure, unless

21

otherwise noted, connotes children who are below the third percentile in height and weight for their age.

This literature review identifies three general groupings of variables, each of which can act as a potent force in causing the retardation of early growth: (1) Nutritional "failure-to-thrive" is commonly identified as the cause of growth failure; (2) Feeding-behavior disturbances can often result in malnutrition but are, primarily, consequences of emotional factors; (3) Non-organic "failure-to-thrive" or "deprivation dwarfism" is the factor concerned with the stunting of growth that occurs despite an adequate nutritional intake. These three factors must be viewed as distinct, but interacting, forces in any consideration of the independent variables contributing to the risk of early growth failure.

Nutritional "Failure-to-Thrive"

Most research concerned with the nutritional "failure-to-thrive" variable and the topic of malnutrition in general deals with the concept of environmental deprivation and attributes the most immediate cause of malnutrition to the lack of essential nutritional foodstuffs. Most often malnutrition is the result of inadequate protein-calorie intake. Studies are in general agreement that a diet that does not provide the minimum requirements of protein and calories, vitamins and minerals will inevitably result in retarded growth. That is, the importance of the quality as well as the quantity of food must be taken into account in assessing the dietary causes of growth failure. A diet poor in quantity or quality of essential nutrients will cause a child to be small for his or her age, to have the body composition of a much younger child, and to be increasingly susceptible to the effects of infection and disease.

Minimum requirements for the adequate development of children, however, are not known. The Recommended Dietary Allowance put out by the Committee on Dietary Allowance, a subcommittee of the Food and Nutrition Board of the National Research Council, is not "minimal" or even "optimal" for that matter. Dr. Roslyn B. Alfin-Slater pointed out the limitations of the Recommended Dietary Allowance: "It's something above minimum, but we don't really know how much. We know that it is not a minimum requirement. Populations have survived on lesser amounts of nutrients, but this recommendation (RDA) keeps almost all children in good health." Dr. Ernesto Pollitt stated that there is not as much information as we need, attributing this to an over-emphasis on protein calorie deficiency and its possible effect on behavior and mental development.

22

Although the minimum requirements may not be readily specifiable, there is considerable information on the effects of specific deficiencies. One kind of deficiency whose commonness was generally agreed upon by experts interviewed was iron deficiency. Iron deficiency in this country is estimated to be extensive and its potential effects on mental development are of concern, as well as its better-known effects on physical performance. The effects of iron deficiency on maintenance of attention and the effect of attention span on school performance can create a number of serious problems for children. It should be noted that iron deficiency that has not reached the stage of iron deficiency anemia is not likely to be recognized or treated. Thus, iron deficiency is a clear example of a known harm to children that is probably affecting large numbers of American children but is not so extreme as other forms of undernutrition and therefore not often recognized.

Even though efforts have been made to identify significant demographic variables predisposing toward malnutrition, most studies have been primarily concerned with assessing the long-term developmental effects of early malnutrition. Special attention has been given to the possibility and degree of later catch-up growth. Two opposing theories on the permanent effect of early malnutrition have developed. Assuming that there is an early critical period for physical development, growth failure during that period will result in permanent stunting and minimal catch-up growth even in the most optimal environmental conditions. If, on the other hand, there is no such critical period, then full catch-up growth will occur when essential environmental conditions are present.

Several studies support the hypothesis that early malnutrition has an irreversible effect. MacCarthy and Booth (1970) attempted to gain some insight into the etiology of growth failure in ten children by investigating their social backgrounds and parental attitudes and by considering relevant findings of other studies. They hypothesized that since the rate of growth during the first year of life is greater than at any other period, retarded growth during this early period due to nutritional deprivation may have a permanent effect on subsequent growth.

Chase and Martin (1970) compared 19 children who had been hospitalized with undernutrition in the first year of life with a matched control group three to four years later on a number of developmental indices. Their results showed the test group to be lower in height, weight, head circumference, and developmental quotient than the controls, thus suggesting that undernutrition in the first year of life is detrimental to later development. Furthermore, impairment

of physical and mental development appeared to be correlated with the duration
of undernutrition in the first year of life. Nine children treated in the first
four months of age had at the time of follow-up a mean developmental quotient of
95 (similar to that of the controls), whereas the ten children with undernutrition after four months of age had a higher frequency of low indices for height,
weight, and head circumference, and a mean developmental quotient at follow-up
of 70. Chase and Martin also identified a number of social factors associated
with undernutrition, including parental separation, numerous young siblings,
alcohol-related problems, and inadequate money. Their study gives limited support to the critical period theory; however, it must be noted that since the
children were returned to the original home environment, it is not known whether
they would have fared better in a different environment.

Overall, most studies tend to agree with the principle of catch-up growth,
rather than with the concept of the irreversibility of early malnutrition. In a
five year longitudinal study of 100 infants and children who had been admitted
with severe malnutrition to the British American Hospital in Lima, Peru, Graham
(1972) found that children have a seemingly unlimited potential for catch-up
growth and that adequate nutrition in a healthy environment can eliminate the
effects of early, severe malnutrition on linear and head growth. His results
suggested that the stunting demonstrated by such children is largely the result
of continued undernutrition during most of the entire growth period.

In an extensive review of some of the relevant research, Hansen et al.
(1971) concluded that nutritional growth retardation could imply a good prognosis given proper treatment and a continuing improved environment. They presented
evidence showing successful dietary therapy in cases of growth retardation to be
characterized by growth rates two to three times above normal for the child's
age. Retarded growth and small adult stature, they proposed, may be seen as an
adaptation to a prolonged restricted diet.

Both the deleterious effects of malnutrition and the rehabilitative effects of treatment are more pronounced the earlier they occur in a child's life.
Prader, Tanner, and von Harnack (1963) did a longitudinal study of five children
whose growth had been retarded by inadequate nutritional intake resulting from
starvation and severe illness. Their results showed that the children's growth
rates accelerated considerably during and following recovery. Furthermore, the
rapid phase of growth continued until the children had caught up to their normal
growth curve. On the basis of other related research, it was pointed out, however, that the degree to which the growth rate is successful in regaining its

original curve depends on the length of time for which growth has been slowed. In a review of a number of empirical studies dealing with the regulation of human growth, Tanner (1963) noted that even if a child's natural growth rate is slowed by acute malnutrition, as soon as the missing food or nutrients are supplied again, the child catches up with its original curve. If the period of growth arrest by malnutrition or starvation is prolonged, however, the catch-up growth will be incomplete.

In an overview of the issue of nutritional "failure-to-thrive," several environmental variables are identified as highly associated with early malnutrition and growth retardation. The most basic of these is the amount of money that is or can be spent on the feeding of a family's children. Related to this is the mother's marital status, her educational level, her health, her knowledge of nutritional needs, and the family density. Early and prolonged malnutrition is likely to result in at least some impairment of physical development and contributes to the risk of illness and disease. But if adequate nutrition and a "healthy" environment are provided soon enough, growth-retarded children have a strong potential for catch-up growth. In general, then, the long-term developmental effects of nutritional "failure-to-thrive" appear to depend on at least two parameters: how long the malnutrition lasts during the child's growth period and how early in the child's life malnutrition occurs.

Feeding Behavior Disturbances

In some cases, early growth failure may be caused by inadequate nutrient intake that is the result of the child's abnormal eating habits. These feeding-behavior disturbances are usually produced by some kind of psychosocial deprivation. Such feeding problems as anorexia, inadequate appetite, food fads, and aversions are generally regarded as personality disorders that have arisen from defects in mother-child interaction. Most investigators assume that the mother is the dominant force in the environment and have therefore attributed such feeding problems to maternal deprivation.

In an epidemiological study in Newcastle-upon-Tyne, England, Brandon (1970) compared a group of 126 maladjusted children with a control group of 105 normal children, paying particular attention to eating behavior disturbances. Using parental interviews, school and hospital records, and individual clinical assessments, he showed that inadequate appetite and food fads were several times more common among the maladjusted group than among the control group. Conflict over toilet training and speech disorders (especially stuttering) were several factors highly associated with incidences of eating disturbance. The investigator attributed these results to defective communication between parent and child. A number of parental factors were also found to be highly associated with eating disturbances, including a high incidence (67 percent) of neurotic disturbance among the mothers, reports by mothers of psychological stress and an unhappy childhood, a poor marital relationship, and an unhappy home atmosphere.

Using a clinical approach, Bentovim (1970) studied the cases of five children suffering from feeding disorders at the Hospital for Sick Children in London. Focusing primarily on persistent difficulties in mother-child relations, he pointed out that the function of feeding is related to social attachment and that by giving, taking, or refusing food, the mother and/or child expressed acceptance or rejection, love or hate. He concluded that certain maternal behavior or anxiety can be misinterpreted by the child and may result in behavioral disturbances that in turn evoke maternal anxiety or rejection. To break this vicious circle of interaction effects, Bentovim suggested that therapy may change the child's perception of food, the behavior of the mother who feeds, and the confusion of the child's own impulses. At the same time, the mother must understand how her actions and communication of anxiety affect the child.

In a descriptive study, Apley et al. (1971) examined the background profiles of 16 children who had no signs of hormonal irregularities but showed impaired growth resulting from food restriction or lack of eating. The study found that arrested growth was often related to events that brought about changes in the relationships within the family; the investigators noted particularly the lack of communication or interaction between mother and child. The results of the study suggest that anxiety in the family can impair social interaction and emotional health, causing disorders in child behavior such as speech and sleep disturbances, enuresis, and under-eating. Apley and his colleagues pointed out that in the diagnosis and treatment of feeding problems, family attitudes may be more important than the state of the child.

Perhaps the most serious and most extreme of the feeding-behavior disturbances is anorexia nervosa. This self-imposed restriction of food intake has been extensively studied by clinicians. It is commonly perceived as a severe psycho-physiological disorder and a potential threat to life. Although there is a general lack of agreement concerning its etiology, several studies have sought an explanation in disorders in the mother-child relationship. Di Cagno and Ravetto (1968) clinically examined 30 children who had clearly non-organic anorexia in the first year of life and an abnormal personality structure that appeared at a later date. The results indicated two different psychopathogenetic patterns. An early form observed in pre-neurotic and neurotic children was attributed to a communication breakdown between mother and infant, in which maternal personality dysfunctions elicited defensive responses in the child (e.g., not eating) that in turn strengthened the anxiety or depression of the mother. The anorexia disappeared or improved when the child was fed by a different person. The second form, which arose mainly in the second trimester of the first year, was observed in psychotic children and constituted a form of aggressive protest on the part of the infant toward a non-accepting mother-figure. Di Cagno and Ravetto suggested that early recognition is the key to effective therapeutic intervention that can restore communication between mother and child.

Caldston (1974) clinically evaluated 50 children hospitalized for anorexia nervosa and reported that all of the patients had deliberately decided not to eat because of two ideas with which they were obsessed: one was that they were too fat; the other was that eating was bad. He found that the parents supported their children's renunciation or oral pleasure through approval of dieting and non-recognition of the children's weight loss. Furthermore, the parents had promoted both consciously and unconsciously the child's obsession for perfection.

These clinical studies generally lack rigorous empiricism and operationality and have often been based on small samples. They have tended, in addition, to focus only on the mother-child dyad and hence have not sought information about other factors or persons impinging on the mother or child. These studies do, however, shed some light on the potential contribution of parental roles in the etiology of childhood feeding-behavior.

Non-Organic "Failure-to-Thrive"

Growth impairment can usually be directly attributed to some form of nutritional deprivation, but many children fail to gain weight at normal rates despite adequate nutritional intake. Such non-organic "failure-to-thrive" is believed to result from psychosocial or emotional deprivation, because when these children are transferred to an adequate emotional environment, they usually resume a normal rate of growth. Although a number of terms in such an issue are difficult to operationalize, several studies have attempted to clarify the physiological mechanisms and the associated psychosocial factors.

A review of a number of studies dealing with "deprivation dwarfism" led Gardner (1972) to postulate the existence of a physiological pathway where environmental deprivation and emotional disturbance might affect the endocrine apparatus and thereby have an impact on a child's growth. He pointed out that centers in the hypothalamus that control emotions are intricately involved with hormonal release in the pituitary gland. Emotions can thus affect levels of blood sugar, growth hormone, and stimulation of stomach secretion. He also noted evidence from recent research theorizing the existence of a cause-and-effect relationship between deprivation dwarfism and abnormal patterns of sleep in the emotionally-deprived child. In their longitudinal study of ten growth-retarded children, MacCarthy and Booth (1970) noted substantial growth failure in the absence of malnutrition and referred to several studies showing that gastric secretion rates are intimately integrated with the total behavior responses of infants. They also pointed out, like Gardner, that there is strong evidence that emotional disturbances can impinge on hypothalamic functioning and thus impair hormonal releases of the pituitary. A similar theory was advanced by Frasier and Rallison (1972) when they noted that a five-and-a-half-year-old, emotionally-deprived girl failed to resume normal growth rates when injected with growth hormone. They hypothesized that relative resistance to growth hormone may play a significant role in the growth failure associated with emotional deprivation. Thus, the exact mechanism is unknown, but it is generally agreed that emotional factors can, and often do, affect growth through physiological channels.

Several studies have undertaken extensive psychological investigations of the various factors that constitute psychosocial deprivation and cause non-organic "failure-to-thrive." Evans, Rinehart, and Succop (1972) studied the maternal and family background variables of 40 children who were admitted with non-organic growth failure to the Children's Hospital of Pittsburgh. A number of characteristics were found to be related to prognosis, including: whether the living conditions were good; whether the physical care of the child was good; whether the maternal affect was one of depression, anger, or hostility toward the child; whether there were chronic losses revealed in the history of the mother; whether the mother perceived the child as ill, retarded, or "bad;" and how strained or unsure the mother-child interaction was. The study stressed the necessity of child protection and concomitant family treatment methods to assess and amend the already-existing caretaking capacities, rather than mere reliance on removal of the child from the family.

Fischhoff, Whitten, and Pettit (1971) used a psychiatric assessment of the personalities of 12 mothers with children showing non-organic growth failure within the first two years of life. Ten of the 12 mothers were classified as having "character disorders." Some of the basic features they observed were disturbed early childhood histories, limited capacity for abstraction or planning for the future, the use of denial, isolation, and projection as major mechanisms of defense, and a predisposition toward action or acting out as opposed to thought. The mothers with "character disorders" showed a limited ability to perceive and assess accurately the environment, their own needs, or the needs of their children and were limited in ability to adapt to changes in the environment. The study pointed out that although verbal discussion should not be neglected or avoided, mothers suffering from such "character disorders" are more likely to respond to intervention involving action.

Similar features were identified by Togut, Allen, and Lelchuk (1969) in a psychological evaluation of the mothers of nine infants with non-organic growth impairment. The mothers reported emotionally disturbed childhoods, had poor control over their impulses, especially with regard to sex and aggression, tended to project feelings of hostility on to their husbands and children, felt rejected by males, expressed feelings of distress and entrapment in raising their children without adequate emotional or economic support, and showed a high level of anxiety and insecurity. The investigators attributed the presence of these psychological characteristics to numerous children in the immediate family closely spaced and below school age, family instability, low income, poor housing, and social disorder and economic deprivation in the mothers' backgrounds.

In an overview of the issue of non-organic "failure-to-thrive," it is clear that children's growth can be influenced by their emotional status. Within a healthy and stable emotional environment, children's growth rates can return to normal but remain there only if they are not subjected to more psychosocial deprivation.

Summary

Several environmental variables have been identified as predisposing toward the risk of early growth failure. Perhaps the most distinct are: inadequate money to spend on food, parental marital strife, inadequate knowledge of the essential nutrients needed for normal growth, lack of communication or understanding between the mother and child, maternal emotional or psychological instability, a large number of young children in the same family, and an unhappy home atmosphere. There is certainly no invariant relationship between these factors and growth impairment, but they can contribute to an environment in which the nutritional and emotional needs of children are not met.

In spite of the _prima_ _facie_ nature of growth failure as harmful to children's development, many issues remain unsolved or controversial. Etiologic factors are confounded. While nutritional intake is a direct antecedent of some types of growth failure, low nutritional intake in the case of feeding problems is a result of emotional and psychological factors of a less clear etiologic nature. In the studies cited here that sought such etiologic explanations, the non-specific nature of the enormous number of variables investigated and the relatively small numbers of cases sampled render the works inconclusive. Controversy surrounds the reversibility of the effects of early growth failure, in part reflecting ambiguities in the interaction between nutritional and non-nutritional environmental factors. Given these kinds of ambiguities and uncertainties, it seems premature to rush to any conclusions about such vaguely defined and poorly operationalized concepts as "maternal deprivation" as known determinants of early growth failure. Thus, while nutritional intake and growth rates are relatively clear and reliably measured variables, the interaction of less well-defined phenomena, which are infinitely more difficult to operationalize, limits our understanding and explanation of the multifaceted problem of early growth failure.

Childhood and Adolescent Obesity

The risk of obesity is at the opposite end of the growth continuum from early growth failure. Contrary to what some might think, obesity is a greater problem than underweight in impoverished areas. The immediate harm to children of being fat may be somewhat speculative at this time, but the association of obesity with other diseases in later life does place it at least within the category of potentially harmful. The origins of obesity do not seem to be well understood. Some obesity may be congenital; some may be due to very early feeding training; some may reflect an impaired caretaker-child relationship. Some obesity may actually be a reflection of neglectful feeding practices such as skipped or irregular meals, where children are left to feed themselves or to find food that usually tends to be fattening and unnutritional.

It is difficult to demarcate what is harmful to children in the area of nutrition when global questions are asked about minimal requirements or adequate total diet. What is of interest is the fact that harm cannot be specified in a linear way, e.g., the more food, the better off the child. Harm can result from obesity and there are even problems with the over-administration of vitamins, such as vitamin A. Thus, demarcating harm with respect to nutrition really involves specifying a range between undernutrition and overnutrition.

Although there is little doubt that obesity is a common nutritional disorder, its long-range consequences have not been adequately explained. There is general agreement that obesity can lead to serious social and personality problems (Sarason, 1972), and it is commonly thought that there is an increased risk of heart attacks associated with obesity. The extent to which obesity is actually regarded as a serious problem will, of course, depend upon particular social and cultural attitudes. Furthermore, actions that result in excessive growth and obesity may not be considered neglectful. Attempting to avoid such areas of controversy, this discussion views obesity as an area of risk, and, treating it as a dependent variable, attempts to identify parental and environmental factors with which it is associated. We have not included those studies concerned with the genetic or metabolic factors that predispose to obesity, which are less amenable to environmental intervention.

Accurate figures for the incidence and long-range consequences of obesity are unavailable, due in part to the lack of agreement about its definition and to the variations in methodology and standards of measurement used in much of the relevant research. The majority of studies reviewed in this discussion have purported to deal with the issue of obesity without offering any operational definition for the term; they have viewed its definition as intuitive. Others have presented the "usual" definition of obesity as body weight that is at least 20 percent greater than the standard weights in height-weight tables (Sarason, 1972; Mellbin and Vuille, 1973). On the other hand, Knittle (1971) has proposed that "obesity" be limited to an excessive deposition and storage of fat as distinguished from "overweight," which does not necessarily imply fatness. Whether obesity refers to overweight or to excessive fatness, it is still considered a potential health risk.

Childhood Obesity

Research in the area of childhood and adolescent obesity can be grouped according to the different stages of life on which it focuses. Studies have searched for possible "causes" as well as investigating the prognosis of obesity at each of the different stages of a child's life. There is general agreement that excessive food intake is the primary contributing factor to obesity, but some theorists have claimed that it is biologically mediated by excessive birth weight. Nisbett and Gurwitz (1970) investigated the eating behaviors highly associated with human obesity in 42 newborn infants from three different birth weight groups. Using an experimental method, they examined the response of the infants to the taste of food (in terms of sweetness) and to the necessity to exert effort in obtaining it (mediated by smaller nipple-hole sizes). Their results showed that the heavy infants responded to taste with increased food intake and were less willing to exert effort to obtain food than were the lighter infants. The investigators drew parallels between their results and the known eating behaviors of obese children and adults, claiming that excessive birth weight may be an early determining factor for obesity.

Contrary evidence was noted by Knittle (1971) in a review accompanying his study of childhood obesity. He cited research showing that the birth weights of children who later become obese are normal, thus indicating that early obesity is due to environmental factors during the first years of life.

Fomon (1971) investigated the relationship between obesity and early feeding practices and diet. He concluded that bottle-fed babies grow more rapidly than breast-fed babies because bottle-fed babies are often encouraged to consume more food and because commercially prepared formulas are higher in caloric content. He also cited evidence that the frequency of feeding has important metabolic consequences. In particular, widely spaced males (characteristic of formula-feeding) are associated with a tendency to obesity. Fomon pointed out that, although a pattern of feeding infants and small children at infrequent intervals is convenient for parents, there is little to suggest that it is nutritionally desirable.

Oates (1973) interviewed 100 mothers of obese infants under six months of age, paying particular attention to the feeding techniques they used. His results showed that 26 of the mothers changed their infants' milk in the first two weeks after birth and that multiple changes were common; that 22 mothers were preparing a milk formula more concentrated than the recommended strength; that the usual age for starting solid feeding was between three and four weeks; and that the practice of adding cereal to the bottle was common. Oates noted evidence from other studies that overfeeding and the early introduction of cereals may contribute to obesity, which in turn is correlated with increased susceptibility to respiratory infections in infancy and excess weight in later childhood.

Shenker, Fisichelli, and Lang (1974) compared the weight of 38 infants of obese foster mothers with the weight of 28 infants of non-obese foster mothers during the first year of life. The infants of obese foster mothers weighed significantly more than the infants of non-obese foster mothers, even though both groups originally weighed the same. The investigators suggested that there is a greater tendency for overweight foster mothers to overfeed their infants.

In his study of the morphology of adipose tissue in obese children, Knittle (1971) noted evidence that early obesity increases the number and size of adipose cells and that childhood obesity is often a forerunner of obesity in adult life. He further noted that overnutrition is the most frequent cause for such cellularity increases.

Most of the studies conclude that overfeeding in infancy leads to later obesity, but there are results that refute this hypothesis. In Sweden, Mellbin and Vuille (1973) did a cross-sectional and longitudinal survey of 972 seven-year-old boys and girls to find out how many obese children in a representative sample of school children had rapidly gained weight as infants and how many of such infants eventually became obese. Their results showed that: (1) 23 percent of the height variation in both sexes was explained by growth patterns during infancy; (2) weight was an inefficient indicator for height variation; (3) on the basis of weight data from the first year, girls did not show a significantly increased risk of becoming obese before the age of seven, but boys stood a 70 percent chance of becoming obese. The investigators concluded that the results of this longitudinal study did not support the hypothesis that infant overfeeding is an important cause of obesity among Swedish urban children.

Adolescent Obesity

Research on adolescent obesity has in general emphasized the importance of childhood growth and obesity. In a longitudinal study, Broverman et al. (1964) analyzed the relation between pre- and post-adolescent body dimensions and growth of 67 boys during adolescence. Their results indicated that pre-adolescent body dimensions contributed more towards post-adolescent body dimensions than did growth during adolescence. A logical interpretation of these findings is that childhood obesity is a likely cause of adolescent obesity.

One of the most comprehensive investigations of adolescent obesity was an interdisciplinary study by Hammar et al. (1973). Ten obese and ten non-obese adolescents were given a battery of psychological tests as well as medical and anthropometric examinations. They and their mothers were also interviewed by a nutritionist, a social worker, and a psychologist. Infant feeding problems, food intolerances, formula changes, and an early introduction of solid foods were found to be characteristic of the obese group. It was also common practice for the parents consistently to use food, particularly sweets, to reinforce good behavior. Although the total daily caloric intake at adolescence was not different between the groups, the obese subjects were less physically active and more interested in sedentary activity. The obese subjects also seemed to be less psychologically well-adjusted than the non-obese subjects. Defective body-image development, low self-esteem, depression, and social isolation were characteristic of the obese group. The obese adolescents were often a focus of parental conflicts, a source of embarrassment, and a scapegoat for their siblings. In addition, the parents tended to view the prognosis for successful weight reduction as hopeless and offered only minimal support in that direction. The investigators suggested that treatment of adolescent obesity should take a strongly therapeutic approach, especially in the more pronounced cases and in those lacking sufficient motivation to succeed under conventional methods, and often should involve the parents and other family members.

Summary

In summary, it appears that early overnutrition can be associated with rapid weight gain and later obesity. Although it seems that childhood obesity is often a forerunner of adolescent obesity, it is not clear whether both are related to infant feeding behaviors. It is only clear that early overfeeding and excessive dietary provisions may bring risk of later obesity. There is little documentation of specific consequences of obesity, but there appears to be general agreement that it can result in serious social, psychological, and physical problems. It must be decided on an individual basis whether actions that result in excessive growth and obesity do indeed constitute neglect. The form of malnutrition manifested by obesity has attracted scant, if any, attention as an element of child neglect. Yet, in view of the impact on child and adolescent and the potential risks in adult life, obesity seems to be a negative factor in a child's general welfare.

REFERENCES

Apley, J., J. Davies, D. R. Davis, and B. Silk. "Nonphysical causes of dwarf-ism." Proceedings of the Royal Society of Medicine, 64, 1971, pp. 135-138.

Bentovim, A. "The clinical approach to feeding disorders of childhood." Journal of Psychosomatic Research, 14, 1970, pp. 267-276.

Brandon, S. "An epidemiological study of eating disturbances." Journal of Psychosomatic Research, 14, 1970, pp. 253-257.

Broverman, D. M., et al. "Physique and growth in adolescence." Child Development, 35, 1964, pp. 857-870.

Chase, H. P. "The effects of intrauterine and postnatal undernutrition on normal brain development." Annals of the New York Academy of Sciences, 205, 1973, pp. 231-244.

Chase, H. P. and H. P. Martin. "Undernutrition and child development." New England Journal of Medicine, 282, 1970, pp. 933-939.

De Hirsch, K., J. Jansky and W. S. Langford. "Comparisons between prematurely and maturely born children at three age levels." American Journal of Orthopsychiatry, 36, 1966, pp. 616-628.

Di Cagno, L. and F. Ravetto. "Anorexia in the first year of life as an expression of changes in the mother-child relationship." Panminerva Medica, 10, 1968, pp. 465-471.

Elmer, E. and G. S. Gregg. "Developmental characteristics of abused children." Pediatrics, 40, 1967, pp. 596-602.

Evans, S. L., J. B. Rinehart, and R. A. Succop. "Failure to thrive: a study of 45 children and their families." Journal of American Academy of Child Psychiatry, 2, 1972, pp. 440-457.

Ferreira, A. J. "Emotional factors in prenatal environment." Journal of Nervous and Mental Disease, 141, 1965, pp. 108-118.

Fischhoff, J., C. F. Whitten, and M. G. Pettit. "A psychiatric study of mothers of infants with growth failure secondary to maternal deprivation." Journal of Pediatrics, 79, 1971, pp. 209-215.

Fomon, S. J. "A pediatrician looks at early nutrition." Bulletin of the New York Academy of Medicine, 47, 1971, pp. 569-578.

Frasier, S. D. and M. L. Rallison. "Growth retardation and emotional deprivation: relative resistance to treatment with human growth hormone." Journal of Pediatrics, 80, 1972, pp. 603-609.

Galdston, R. "Mind over matter: observations on 50 patients hospitalized with anorexia nervosa." Journal of American Academy of Child Psychiatry, 13, 1974, pp. 246-263.

Gardner, L. I. "Deprivation dwarfism." Scientific American, 227, 1972, pp. 76-82.

Graham, G. G. "Environmental factors affecting the growth of children." American Journal of Clinical Nutrition, 25, 1972, pp. 1184-1188.

Hammar, S. L., M. M. Campbell, V. A. Campbell, N. L. Moores, C. Sareen, F. J. Gareis, and B. Lucas. "An interdisciplinary study of adolescent obesity." Journal of Pediatrics, 80, 1972, pp. 373-383.

Hansen, J. D. L., C. Freesemann, A. D. Moodie, and E. D. Evans. "What does nutritional growth retardation imply?" Pediatrics, 47, 1971, pp. 299-311.

Katz, C. and P. M. Taylor. "The incidence of low birth weight in children with severe mental retardation." American Journal of Diseases of Children, 114, 1967, pp. 80-87.

Klein, M. and L. Stern. "Low birth weight and the battered child syndrome." American Journal of Diseases of Children, 122, 1971, pp. 15-18.

Knittle, J. L. "Childhood obesity." Bulletin of the New York Academy of Medicine, 47, 1971, pp. 579-589.

Krieger, I. "Food restriction as a form of child abuse in ten cases of psychosocial deprivation dwarfism." Clinical Pediatrics, 13, 1974, pp. 127-133.

Lubchenco, L. O., M. Delivoria-Papadopoulos, and D. Searls. "Long-term follow-up studies of prematurely born infants. II. Influence of birth weight and gestational age on sequelae." Journal of Pediatrics, 80, 1972, pp. 509-512.

MacCarthy, D. and E. M. Booth. "Parental rejection and stunting of growth." Journal of Psychosomatic Research, 14, 1970, pp. 259-265.

Matheny, A. P. and A. M. Brown. "The behavior of twins: effects of birth weight and birth sequence." Child Development, 42, 1971, pp. 251-257.

Mellbin, T. and J. C. Vuille. "Physical development at seven years of age in relation to velocity of weight gain in infancy with special reference to incidence of overweight." British Journal of Preventive Social Medicine, 27, 1973, pp. 225-235.

Metcoff, J., T. Yoshida, M. Morales, et al. "Biomolecular studies of fetal malnutrition in maternal leukocytes." Pediatrics, 47, 1971, pp. 180-191.

Miller, H. C. and K. Hassanein. "Fetal malnutrition in white newborn infants: maternal factors." Pediatrics, 52, 1973, pp. 504-512.

Naeye, R. L., W. Blanc, and C. Paul. "Effects of maternal nutrition on the human fetus." Pediatrics, 52, 1973, pp. 494-503.

Naeye, R. L., W. Blanc, W. LeBlanc, and M. A. Kratamee. "Fetal complications of maternal heroin addition: abnormal growth, infections and episodes of stress." Journal of Pediatrics, 83, 1973, pp. 1055-1061.

Nisbett, R. E. and S. B. Gurwitz. "Weight, sex, and eating behavior of human newborns." Journal of Comparative and Physiological Psychology, 73, 1970, pp. 245-253.

Oates, R. K. "Infant feeding practices." British Medical Journal, 2, 1973, pp. 762-764.

Ottinger, D. R. and J. E. Simmons. "Behavior of human neonates and prenatal maternal anxiety." Psychological Reports, 14, 1964, pp. 391-394.

Prader, A., J. M. Tanner, and G. A. von Harnack. "Catch-up growth following illness or starvation. An example of developmental canalization in man." Journal of Pediatrics, 62, 1963, pp. 646-659.

Robinson, N. M. and H. B. Robinson. "A follow-up study of children of low birth weight and control children at school age." Pediatrics, 35, 1965, pp. 425-433.

Sarason, I. G. Abnormal Psychology: The Problem of Maladaptive Behavior. New York: Meredith Corp., 1972, pp. 442-444.

Shenker, I. R., V. Fisichelli, and J. Lang. "Weight differences between foster infants of overweight and non-overweight foster mothers." Journal of Pediatrics, 84, 1974, pp. 715-719.

Stein, Z., M. Susser, G. Saenger, and F. Marolla. "Nutrition and mental performance." Science, 178, 1972, pp. 708-713.

Sussman, S. "Narcotic and methamphetamine use during pregnancy: effect on newborn infants." American Journal of Diseases of Children, 106, 1963, pp. 325-330.

Tanner, J. M. "The regulation of human growth." Child Development, 34, 1963, pp. 817-846.

Togut, M. R., J. E. Allen, and L. Lelchuck. "A psychological exploration of the nonorganic failure-to-thrive syndrome." Developmental Medicine and Child Neurology, 11, 1969, pp. 601-607.

Wiener, G. "The relationship of birth weight and length of gestation to intellectual development at ages 8-10 years." Journal of Pediatrics, 76, 1970, pp. 694-699.

Wiener, G., R. V. Rider, W. C. Oppel, L. K. Fischer, and P. A. Harper. "Psychological correlates of low birth weight at six to seven years of age." Pediatrics, 35, 1965, pp. 434-442.

Willerman, L. and J. A. Churchill. "Intelligence and birth weight in identical twins." Child Development, 38, 1967, pp. 623-629.

Williams, M. L. and S. Scarr. "Effect of short term intervention on performance in low birth-weight, disadvantaged children." Pediatrics, 47, 1971, pp. 289-298.

Young, L. Wednesday's Children. New York: McGraw-Hill, 1964.

CHAPTER 5

MENTAL DEVELOPMENT

Thus far we have discussed the research in the field of child development that is primarily concerned with physical aspects of development. The bulk of child development research falls into this category because deficiencies in physical development are more visible and immediately recognizable. We turn now to a discussion of the factors that contribute to deficient mental development.

This area of inquiry has grown during the past two decades in the wake of widespread use of intelligence testing for diagnostic monitoring and selection purposes. With the standardization of such intelligence tests as the Stanford-Binet, Gesell, Cattell, and WISC, the fields of psychology, sociology, and education have increasingly relied upon and implemented simple indices of children's mental development. Such tests have been repeatedly criticized on the grounds of their uncertain external validity, their excessive emphasis on language skills, and their primary reference to white, middle-class norms, but they continue to serve as the major instruments in measuring mental development. Their use has enabled a large number of theorists to treat mental growth as a dependent variable and to investigate factors contributing to mental subnormality. We take such an approach in this discussion in an attempt to identify areas of neglect that affect mental development.

Research on deficient mental development has dealt with a wide spectrum of dependent variables or outcomes for children. The range literally is from death to an increase of seven I.Q. points. Where in that range does one begin to specify or demarcate "harm," and on what basis?

Many of the experts consulted stressed the importance of the inanimate environment in children's cognitive development. Toys, particularly those that stimulate fantasy with children, contribute to the development of their capacity for imaginative thought and abstraction. With reference to neglect, it was pointed out by Dr. Edith Grotberg that:

> More and more we are finding that there are certain
> requirements in the inanimate environment for good
> cognitive development. There can be neglect if the
> child doesn't have what we call 'variety play materi-
> als,' or different kinds of play materials, that are
> sufficiently complex for his age level and have many
> parts. Responsiveness is another important aspect

39

of inanimate objects; objects that will do something
when the child plays with them, like squeak or change
shape, are also important in stimulating mental development.

An equally important stress was put on the positive effects that have been
obtained in programs of parent involvement where parents have been taught about
child development and how to stimulate their children. Outcomes of such studies
are usually measured on a variety of developmental scales and a long-range primary goal with respect to young children is environmental and parental stimulation on their academic achievement.

Relating these ideas to the concept of harm is controversial. What are
the long-range effects on children from lack of stimulation at home? Two lines
of thought emerge here; either they eventually "catch up" if placed in a suitable
school environment or they suffer from an irreversible developmental lag. In
the latter case, they may begin to accelerate their learning rate and eventually
continue at the same rate as others, but because of their initial lag, they will
always be behind.

We have chosen to focus upon the salient independent variables that seem
most relevant to the issue of child neglect as factors of early trauma: the effects of low birth weight, undernutrition, abuse, and early stress on mental development. Maternal and paternal influences and the impact of institutionalization are also examined as "caretaking" variables. Instead of trying to demonstrate an absolute cause-and-effect relationship between these factors and deficient mental development, this discussion concentrates on identifying factors
that may be associated with, or may contribute to, the risk of mental subnormality.

Low Birth Weight

Low birth weight may be a result of intrauterine undernutrition, but can
also be associated with a number of different antecedent factors (for a more
thorough discussion of low birth weight, see the previous section on physical
development). Evidence cited by Chase (1973) with reference to intrauterine undernutrition shows that prenatal nutritional deficiency can be significantly associated with the impairment of intellectual development and the retardation of
brain growth. Chase noted that due to the large number of possible postnatal
influences in such cases, it is speculative to single out the factor of prenatal
undernutrition.

Stein et al. (1972) approached this problem by investigating the effect

of intrauterine undernutrition on the later intellectual performance of a cohort
sample of 125,000 males who had been prenatally exposed to the 1944-45 famine
in Holland. Because of the distinct specificity of the Dutch famine both in
time and in space, the abundant information on type and degree of nutritional
deprivation, and the great size of the sample, such a study enabled isolation of
the effect of intrauterine undernutrition on mental development from other ele-
ments of the social environment. The results showed a significant reduction in
the birth weights of the sample in comparison with a population not exposed to
famine. Neither IQ scores nor the frequency of mental retardation in the study
sample, however, showed evidence of an association between intrauterine undernutrition (or low birth weight) and deficient mental development. Caution must
be utilized in interpreting these ex post facto findings. Women who were able
to bring their pregnancies to full term during such trying circumstances may
have had some altered circumstances and/or characteristics that differentiated
them from other women.

Other studies on the issue of low birth weight and mental development
have avoided the limitations of looking only at prenatal undernutrition. Willerman and Churchill (1967) administered the WISC to 27 sets of identical twins,
five to fifteen years of age, and found that the twin with the lower birth weight
had lower verbal and performance IQ scores than did the heavier twin sibling.
Furthermore, this birth weight-IQ relationship was demonstrated in both a group
of white middle-class twins and in a racially mixed lower SES group selected on
the basis of poor school performance. In a longitudinal study, De Hirsch, Jansky, and Langford (1966) compared 53 children of birth weights below 2,500 gm.
with 53 children of full-term births on the basis of academic performance tests
at kindergarten, first grade, and second grade levels. Although all of the subjects had been selected as exhibiting IQ levels within the normal range, the results showed that the low birth weight children performed significantly less well
than did the controls at all age levels. The investigators interpreted their
results to mean that because the normal stages of infantile growth are delayed
in low birth weight children, they suffer learning deficiencies in the early
school years.

Wiener in separate investigations (Wiener et al., 1965; Wiener, 1970) in
an on-going longitudinal study found corroborating evidence. Controlling for
the factors of race, social class, and maternal attitudes and practices and using tests of psychological and intellectual development, Wiener examined 442 low
birth weight children at six to seven years of age and 417 of these children at

eight to ten years of age, and compared their scores to a matched control group of 405 full-term children of similar age and size. The results showed that the low birth weight children had significantly lower test scores than the controls. Furthermore, the degree of psychological and intellectual impairment appeared to increase with decreasing birth weight.

In another longitudinal study, Lubchenco et al. (1972) examined 91 ten-year-old children whose birth weights were less than 1,500 gm. on a number of developmental indices. The results showed both weight at birth and gestational age to be associated with the incidence of moderate and severe handicaps at fol-low-up. For example, the highest incidence of handicaps, including learning disorder, occurred in the smallest infants of shortest gestational age, whereas the lowest incidence occurred in infants of 1,450 gm. at birth and 33 weeks gestation.

Such evidence seems to support the notion that low birth weight may be associated with deficient mental development. Nonetheless, there exists evidence that makes the issue controversial. Robinson and Robinson (1965) did a comprehensive follow-up study of eight to ten-year-old children. The birth weights of 33 of them were 1,500 gm. or less, of 102 were between 1,501 and 2,500 gm., and of 92 more than 2,500 gm. Their results showed that the two groups of low birth weight children did not fare any less well on a number of indices, including IQ, than did the children of normal birth weight, except for what might have been expected from a knowledge of their social class backgrounds.

Postulating that the deleterious effects of low birth weight on intellectual development may be due to the inadequate early stimulation that normally accompanies the isolation of newborn premature infants, Scarr-Salapatek and Williams (1973) experimentally studied the effects of early stimulation on 30 consecutively-born, low birth weight infants. All of the infants weighed between 1,300 and 1,800 gm. at birth and were alternately assigned to experimental and control groups. The 15 infants in the control group received normal newborn care for premature infants. The two groups were assessed at one week and four weeks with the Brazelton Cambridge Newborn Scales, at one year on the Cattell Infant Intelligence Scale, and were observed as to infant and caretaker behaviors. They found that at four weeks the early stimulation program was effective in promoting behavioral development, and at one year the experimental group had significantly higher developmental quotients and IQ's than did the control group. Furthermore, better development within the experimental group was shown to be related to more maternal play stimulation.

In sum, low birth weight, especially in interaction with postnatal environmental factors, may be a precursor of impaired mental development. It seems doubtful, however, on the basis of the evidence provided by Stein et al. (1972), that prenatal undernutrition is the all-important factor. In view of the evidence given by Scarr-Salapatek and Williams (1973), there may be an early critical period for sensory stimulation in terms of mental development. The most salient factor in the mental subnormality of many low birth weight children may be the fact that they were isolated immediately following birth and may thus have been deprived of necessary early stimulation.

Undernutrition

Many investigators in recent years have tried to show that early undernutrition has a permanent retarding effect on mental development or capacity. The issue is of obvious socio-political importance in view of the high incidence of infant undernutrition throughout the world. Some recent evidence has indicated that severe malnutrition in the first year of life is associated with reduction of growth of the brain and thus may be indirectly related to lower intelligence.

In an extensive review of empirical studies dealing with the effects of early undernutrition on brain development, Chase (1973) cited evidence suggesting that both prenatal and early postnatal undernutrition may result in reductions of brain weight and size, brain cellularity, and myelin lipid formation. He noted that the human brain accumulates approximately 25 percent of its weight prior to birth, reaches a peak in rate of growth at birth, and weighs 75 percent of its adult weight by one year of age. This suggests that nutritional insults between birth and one year of age may have the greatest effect on incremental brain weight. He further pointed out that although studies have not assessed the ability of the human brain to recover from undernutrition following rehabilitation, head circumferences have been shown to be low during and following infantile malnutrition and may be closely correlated with brain weight and size.

In a retrospective study, Brown (1965) reviewed 1,094 autopsies of Ugandan children from birth to 15 years of age and analyzed their body and brain weights. He grouped the results by age and divided them according to whether or not the final diagnosis indicated malnutrition. His results showed that the mean brain weight of the malnourished children was significantly lower than that of the well-nourished children. In conclusion, Brown suggested that since human brain growth appears to level off at the age of one year, undernutrition during an early critical period can adversely affect brain growth.

While the Chase (1973) and Brown (1965) studies support the notion that early undernutrition affects brain development, they fail to confront directly the issue of mental development. Brain growth may be related to mental functioning and intelligence. Pollitt (1973) refutes the concept of this relationship by stating that "there is no conclusive evidence that either a slow rate of biochemical maturation or a comparatively small brain at maturity, like that found in malnourished children, is detrimental to intelligence." Thus, evidence of brain growth retardation is not an uncontroverted indicator of deficient mental development; it may be indirectly related, or future evidence may show it to be directly related, to mental growth.

Pollitt (1973) has cautioned against any investigation that fails to make the distinction between two conditions of malnutrition: marasmus and kwashiorkor. Marasmus results from an absence of all kinds of food intake, while kwashiorkor results from protein calorie deficiency. Both conditions are similar in their deleterious effects on intelligence, but differ in their prognosis following treatment for undernutrition. Specifically, the data cited were conclusive in suggesting that marasmus results in more permanent mental impairment. Pollitt proposed that marasmic children are more likely to be permanently impaired because they are more likely to have been exposed for a longer period of time to poor diet, as well as to multiple adverse biosocial factors. On the other hand, according to Pollitt, children suffering from kwashiorkor, who have undergone a severe protein deficiency at a specific time after having had an otherwise healthy development, seem to have a better likelihood of recovering their intellectual potential.

The issue of permanence of damage to mental development is, nonetheless, controversial as can be seen in two reports dealing with the effects of kwashiorkor on mental development. In a longitudinal study in India, Srikantia and Sastri (1971) used intelligence tests to examine and compare 19 children who had been successfully treated for kwashiorkor five to eight years earlier, with a group consisting of three non-malnourished matched controls for each of the 19 subjects. The results showed that the children who once had kwashiorkor performed only half as well as those who did not. Furthermore, re-examination after two years indicated no tendency toward a narrowing of the gap in mental functioning between the two groups.

Contrary results were obtained by Hansen et al. (1971) when they used subject siblings who had not had kwashiorkor as controls in an attempt to stand-

ardize the non-nutritive factors that play a part in the determination of intelligence. Their analysis of the intelligence scores of 40 South African chi-
dren with histories of kwashiorkor nine to ten years previously after the age of
ten months and 40 sibling controls showed no differences between the two groups.
The investigators concluded that an acute, severe nutritional deficiency such as
kwashiorkor occurring after the age of ten months does not have an irreversible
retarding effect on mental development.

In their work in Guatemala, Klein et al. (1972) raised similar questions
about the independent contributions of physical growth and social factors to
cognitive functioning. They compared populations of children adequately nour-
ished through dietary protein-calorie supplement and those not receiving such a
supplement, the vast majority of whom had some form of mild to moderate malnutrition (rather than the more severe kwashiorkor or marasmus suffered by children in the other studies reported). They used head circumference and total
height as indices of nutritional status. Familial social measures included
housing quality, father's occupation, mother's dress, her hygiene practices,
task instruction of children, and number of adult social contacts. The dependent variables of psychological functioning were divided into language facility,
short-term memory for numbers, and perceptual analysis. Although cautious in
their conclusions, the authors reported that it was impossible to separate the
independent contributions to cognitive functioning of physical growth and social
factors. Two major qualifications in their data were that (1) the magnitude of
associations varied widely by cognitive domain and (2) there were major sex differences in the results obtained.

Most of the research dealing with the effects of undernutrition on mental
development has focused on intelligence. As indicated previously, Chase (1973)
suggests that both prenatal and postnatal undernutrition may be associated with
significant intellectual impairment. In a longitudinal study Chase and Martin
(1970) compared 19 children three to four years after being hospitalized with
undernutrition in the first year of life with a matched control group on a number of developmental indices. Their results showed the test group to be lower
than the controls on several indices including IQ, thus suggesting that undernutrition in the first year of life is detrimental to mental development. They
observed, furthermore, that impairment appeared to correlate with the duration
of undernutrition in the first year of life. Nine children treated for undernutrition in the first four months of age had, at the time of follow-up, an average mental development quotient of 95 (on the basis of the Yale Revised De-

45

velopmental Exam), which was similar to that of the controls, whereas the ten children with undernutrition after four months of age had an average mental developmental quotient of 70 at follow-up.

In a comparative study, Richardson, Birch, and Hertzig (1973) found similar results using IQ and WRAT scores, school grades, and teachers' evaluations to examine the school performance of 62 Jamaican boys (five to eleven years old) who had been treated for severe infantile malnutrition in their first two years of life. In comparison with 68 non-malnourished classmates of the same age and sex, the malnourished boys did significantly less well on all four measures of mental development. On the same tests, 31 non-malnourished siblings of the malnourished boys were significantly lower in comparison to their classmates on only WRAT scores; other measures, including IQ scores, showed them to be essentially equal to their classmates. From this it would seem that the undernutrition of the test group was the salient factor associated with intellectual impairment.

In subsequent work, however, Richardson (1974) treated the acute episode of malnutrition as only one of multiple variables that might explain the differences in the functional development of these children. He developed a series of measures covering a gamut of factors that might impinge on the children. These included measures of maternal factors such as reproductive history, maternal upbringing, present capabilities, exposure to mass media, presence of a social network; measures of physical and economic resources of the family; and measures of child-related experience including the diversity of social experiences, amount of intellectual stimulation, amount of schooling, and attendance. Using all these measures, it was found that children who had been hospitalized for malnutrition had a more disadvantaged background on almost every variable. A composite background measure was developed using one item from each of the maternal, economic, and child-related experiences. This composite measure was entered into a multiple regression analysis along with the factor of malnutrition -- the fact of hospitalization -- and the child's height and IQ. The resulting regression equation explained 67 percent of the variance. The smallest contribution to the explained variance was the information about hospitalization. These data lend support to the idea that the effects on mental development of an acute episode of malnutrition can only be understood within the total context of the life of the child in whom it occurs.

In summary, it appears that early undernutrition is associated with the impairment of mental development. It may affect not only intelligence levels but also brain growth. Although the long-range effects of acute episodes of nutritional insult such as kwashiorkor are controversial, it seems conclusive that the prognosis of such early, long-duration nutritional insults as marasmus and other forms of protein-calorie malnutrition may be the permanent impairment of intellectual functioning. Most of these studies have been concerned almost exclusively with the issue of early undernutrition. This focus limits their conclusions, for early undernutrition should not be singled out as the most important factor associated with the retardation of mental development. It must be considered, rather, as part of a much more complex situation.

Other Variables of Early Trauma

In addition to early undernutrition and low birth weight, several other variables have been investigated as factors of early trauma that may be deleterious to mental development. In a longitudinal study, Elmer and Gregg (1967) examined the developmental characteristics of 20 children whose records at the Children's Hospital of Pittsburgh showed them to have been victims of child abuse. The children were found to have extensive physical and emotional problems and to be below normal intelligence levels. Of the 20 children in the study, ten had IQ scores falling below 80 even though several years had passed since the last episode of abuse. In a three-year follow-up study of 25 abused and neglected children, Morse, Sahler, and Friedman (1970) found only 30 percent of the children to be free of physical, intellectual, and emotional problems. Of the 21 children for whom IQ data were available, nine were classified by the investigators as mentally retarded. Although these two studies seem to suggest a poor prognosis in the mental development of abused children, their methodologies failed to clarify whether low IQ followed or preceded abuse.

A few studies have examined the effects of early stress on mental development. Brodie and Winterbottom (1967) investigated the background trauma of eleven children with learning problems and compared them to those of a normal control sample matched on age, IQ, and social class. It was found that the children with learning problems had been subjected to traumatic and stressful events significantly more often than had the controls. Such events included death of a household member, severe illness, separation from parents, and child abuse. Klatskin, McGarry, and Steward (1966) compared the intellectual development during the first year of life of 21 infants scoring below seven on the Apgar scale and judged potentially stressed at birth, with 22 infants who scored higher on the Apgar scale and were thus judged to be normal at birth. Those infants suspected of being cases of neonatal stress showed a significant retardation of physical and mental development in comparison with the "normal" infants. In a longitudinal-correlational study, Werner, Honzik, and Smith (1968) explored the usefulness of psychological and pediatric appraisals of intelligence at 20 months of age in forecasting the mental ability and achievement levels at ten years of age for a sample of 639 full-term children. From their analysis they concluded that a combination of scores on a measure of perinatal-stress, Cattell IQ, social quotient (Vineland), pediatricians rating, and parental SES was the best predictor of ten-year-old IQ (multiple correlation coefficient of .58).

Maternal Behavior

Although much of the relevant research has been concerned with the effects of early trauma on subsequent mental development, many investigators have shown more interest in examining the effects of caretakers on the mental development of the children in their charge. It should be pointed out that in these investigations the dependent variables of intellectual functioning were not in the severe range. In many of these studies differences in the levels of functioning of subjects either were more subtle manifestations of difference or were differences within the more optimal range (e.g., differences among a population all of whom had attained college entrance).

The effects of prenatal maternal experiences upon their children have been investigated by Drillien and Wilkinson (1964) in a retrospective study of 227 mentally defective children (IQ's below 60), of whom 70 were cases of Down's syndrome. There was a significantly higher incidence of severe emotional stress in the pregnancies of mothers giving birth to infants with Down's syndrome than there was among the mothers of non-mongoloid defectives. Regardless of age, the risk of having a child with Down's syndrome was increased about three-fold where the history indicated severe stress in early pregnancy or before conception.

Other theorists have investigated the effects of prenatal maternal anxiety. Davids, Halden, and Gray (1963) administered a battery of psychological tests to 50 pregnant women and assigned them either to a "high anxiety" or a "low anxiety" group. Eight months after childbirth, the women and their infants were seen for psychological assessment. The results showed that the women who were highly anxious during pregnancy received much less favorable personality ratings by an examiner and scored significantly higher on hostility and control factors (as measured by the PARI) at the eight month assessment than did the

48

"low anxious" mothers. Furthermore, the children of the mothers who were low in anxiety during pregnancy received significantly higher developmental quotients on both the Bayley Infant Mental and Motor Scales. The interpretation of these results must be qualified by the reasons for the greater anxiety among one group of mothers. The explanatory variables may well lie in the context of the mothers' anxiety, rather than in anxiety per se.

Several reports have emphasized the importance of maternal behaviors in stimulating mental development. Yarrow (1963) correlated the behavior and IQ ratings of 40 six-month-old infants with assessments of their mothers' inter- actions with them in the areas of need-gratification and tension reduction, pro- vision of stimulation, and affectional-emotional interchange. He found highly significant correlations between most of the maternal care variables and infant developmental progress. The greatest of these correlations was between IQ and the amount and quality of stimulation provided by the mother. Such evidence supports the concept of an early critical period for sensory stimulation in terms of mental development. Willerman and Stafford (1972) examined the rela- tionship between parental intelligence and adolescent intelligence in 104 fami- lies. Their results demonstrated the presence of a maternal effect on the in- tellectual functioning of teenage children by showing that the children more closely resembled the level of intellectual performance of their mothers than of their fathers. In a study of maternal child-rearing behaviors and their ef- fects on the creativity levels of 96 college males, Heilbrun (1971) found that, on the basis of teacher evaluations, scores on the Adjective Check List, and scores on two Guilford creativity tests, high-in-control, low-in-nurturance maternal behaviors resulted in significantly lower levels of creativity among their children than did low-in-control, high-in-nurturance maternal child-rear- ing behaviors.

Thus, it appears from these studies that prenatal maternal traumas and maternal behaviors can significantly influence the mental development of chil- dren as measured by such instruments as the Bayley Infant Mental and Motor Scales and IQ tests.

Paternal Absence

Although most studies have concentrated on maternal effects on child de- velopment, a few have examined paternal effects. The positive effects associa- ted with the presence of the fathers are inferred from the studies that focus on paternal absence. Blanchard and Biller (1971) examined the relationship between

49

father-availability and the academic performance of third-grade boys. Their results showed that the academic performance and achievement of boys with high father presence was significantly higher than the average third grade levels, whereas the performance of boys whose fathers had been absent from before the age of five was significantly lower than the average.

Sutton-Smith, Rosenberg, and Landy (1968) compared the effects of father absence for varying lengths of time and varying developmental periods with the effects of father presence, as reflected in their children's college entrance scores on the ACE. The study sample consisted of 1055 sophomore college students making up two groups: a father-absent group of 295 students and a father-present group of 760 students. The scores for the father-absent group were significantly lower than were those for the father-present group. The effects were more pronounced in males than in females and seemed to interact with the sibling composition of the families. The greatest effects were seen to occur during the early and middle childhood years (zero to nine years of age); boys without brothers were more affected than were those with brothers; girls with a younger brother were more affected than were those without; and only-girls were affected more than were only-boys. The investigators suggested that the effects of father absence on mental development may be due to the disruption of the child's sexual-identification patterns and the compensatory behavior of the mother without a husband.

In another study by the same investigators, Landy, Rosenberg, and Sutton-Smith (1969) examined the effects of limited father absence on the quantitative mathematical performances of 100 females on the ACE. The period and length of time that the father worked on a night shift, thus being unavailable during most of the day, was used as an index of limited father absence. The subjects whose fathers had worked the night shift after they reached the age of ten had significantly higher scores on the college entrance examinations than did the total father-absent group, thus indicating that the ages from one to nine years are a critical period for the development of quantitative skills in girls. The total number of years of night shift work was only significant in differential effect if it lasted about nine years or more. The report suggested that the important dimension to be considered in the relation of partial father absence to cognitive development is the period in the child's life when the absence occurred. On the basis of their results in this study, the investigators discounted their earlier hypothesis that paternal-absence effects may be due to the compensatory behavior of the mother without a husband and concluded instead that paternal absence effects are simply due to the decreased amount of interaction between the father and the child.

Institutionalization

In a large number of studies investigating possible caretaker effects on mental development, special consideration has been given to the issue of institutionalization. This caretaking arrangement obviously exists because it provides a needed service, but the evidence of most reports has focused on the deleterious effects of institutionalization on mental development. In a longitudinal study, Hansen (1971) investigated the short-term developmental effects of infant institutionalization in nursery homes. Hetzer-Buhler developmental tests were administered to 22 infants at six and eight months of age, who were living in nursery homes and to a control group of 22 infants the same age, who were living in their own families. Observations substantiated that the only two marked differences in the living environments were that in the nurseries the emotional bonds between infant and parental figures appeared less intense and that there was a lack of continuity in the relationship in comparison with family life. Test results at six months showed no considerable differences between the two groups, but at eight months the institutionalized infants exhibited significantly lower mental development scores than did the infants living with their families. The report suggested that nursery homes should terminate their care for infants by the time they reach six months of age and that nurses and trainees should be assigned babies in such a way as to assure each infant of a continuous relationship with a single caretaker while in the institution.

In a report for the Institute for Infant Mental Health in Zurich, Switzerland, Meierhofer (1973) examined the developmental effects of institutionalization on 400 babies and small children. The children were found to be characteristically retarded in mental development. An analysis of the influential factors in each institution studied showed that the infants under rationally organized collective nursing had only fleeting contact with any one nurse, were given attention for a total of less than one out of 24 hours, and lacked sufficient mental stimulation.

Similar negative effects of institutionalization were found by Cheyne and Jahoda (1971) in their comparison of the emotional sensitivity and intelligence of children from orphanages and normal homes. In their study 80 orphaned children, six to ten years old, were matched with 80 children the same age in normal homes and were tested for vocabulary, non-verbal intelligence, and recognition of emotion in speech. Although the two groups showed little difference in emotional sensitivity, the orphaned children were significantly lower than the controls in verbal and non-verbal intelligence.

Taylor (1970) studied the concept formation of ten children institutionalized in infancy who were reared in adoptive homes after the age of three. Her results showed the reverse of the normal sequence of conceptual development. Rather than starting with integrated thought at six years of age and progressing to considerable diversity and complexity of thought processes by the age of nine, the study children exhibited the opposite trend. At six, their thought processes showed evidence of diversity and complexity, while at nine, their thought grew constricted and less complex. Taylor interpreted her results to mean that the impact of normal environmental stimuli was immeasurably greater in the preschool years for such deprived institutionalized children than for home-reared children. Tests of conceptual functioning at the age of six, therefore, reflected their attempts to process the overwhelming flow of information to which they were subjected. The regression of concept formation between the ages of six and nine years was necessary to provide a firmer basis upon which to process realistically the vast amount of information at home and at school to which they were required to adjust satisfactorily.

Several reports have shown concern for the increasing trend toward institutionalization of mentally handicapped children. Two studies have investigated the effects of institutionalization on the social and intellectual development of mongoloid children. Shipe and Shotwell (1965) examined the longitudinal development of 42 mongoloid children after their admission to a California state hospital for the retarded. Of the total sample, 25 had been reared in their own homes for at least two years prior to hospital admission and 17 had been placed in specialized state institutions at birth or soon after. The investigators found that the home-reared mongoloids had significantly higher IQ and SQ scores than did the children institutionalized at birth. Furthermore, this superiority persisted even after 18 months of institutionalization at the state hospital.

Stedman and Eichorn (1964) compared the mental, social, and physical development of ten mongoloid infants who were reared at home with that of ten infants who were reared in an "enriched" institutional setting. Results of the comparison showed that the home-reared group was significantly superior to the institution-reared group in terms of scores on the Bayley Mental Scale and the Vineland Social Maturity Scale. The investigators suggested that possible factors contributing to the superiority of the home-reared children may have included the small adult-child ratio in the homes compared to the large size of living groups among the institution-reared children and the greater reinforcement for speech during play that the home-reared children experienced.

Noting that the deleterious effects of institutionalization seem to be associated with the lack of close caretaker-child relationships, Saltz (1973) hypothesized that individualized, affectional relations are crucial for intellectual and social development. He further suggested that such relations could be provided through a part-time "foster-grandparent" program. To test the theory he assigned 81 institutionalized children to one of two groups: 48 experimentals and 33 controls. The experimental group received part-time "mothering" from elderly institutional aides for up to four years. The control group received only normal institutional care. A significant difference in IQ levels was found to favor the experimental group. IQ results and scores on the Vineland Social Maturity Scale, measured repeatedly during the four years of the experiment, indicated that the experimental group experienced average intellectual progress and average progress in development of social competence over long periods of residence in the institution, in striking contrast to other reported findings of extremely low IQs and SQs for institutionalized children.

Contrary to most of the studies that ascribe particular deleterious effects on development to institutional care, evidence does exist in support of institutionalization. In a longitudinal study, Gavrin and Sacks (1963) examined the intellectual functioning of 132 children aged two through seven years who were cared for at Irvington House in New York. In order to ascertain the effect of institutionalization on mental development, they administered intelligence tests to the children upon admission and again at departure. Significant gains in IQ were found, especially among those whose initial IQs had been below 90. Furthermore, the degree of IQ increase was directly related to the duration of stay at the institution. The investigators suggested that many of the children who fell initially into the below-average IQ group were children of normal intelligence who were suffering impairments based on lack of environmental opportunity, emotional difficulties, or both, and that these cases responded favorably to the institutional environment.

Overall, however, evidence seems to suggest that institutional placement during the earliest years of life may affect adversely the mental development of children. The possible influential factors associated with institutionalization and its negative effects include lack of individualized affectional caretaker-child relations, lack of continuity in caretaking, inadequate personalized

53

attention, and lack of sufficient mental stimulation. Of course, it is simplistic to generalize from one study to all institutions. The quality of care, the size of the institution, and the staff-child ratio vary widely from one institution to another. As Saltz's work with foster-grandparents indicated, the often-observed noxious effects of institutions can be mediated through restructuring the relationships in the children's environment. Thus, institutionalization as a global concept may not be a useful variable for study; what is actually needed is a more specific breakdown of the components in institutional life and their relative contribution to retarding optimal development.

REFERENCES

Blanchard, R. W. and H. B. Biller. "Father availability and academic performance among third-grade boys." _Developmental Psychology_, 4, 1971, pp. 301-305.

Brodie, R. D. and M. R. Winterbottom. "Failure in elementary school boys as a function of traumata, secrecy, and derogation." _Child Development_, 38, 1967, pp. 701-711.

Brown, R. E. "Decreased brain weight in malnutrition and its implications." _The East African Medical Journal_, 42, 1965, pp. 584-595.

Chase, H. P. "The effects of intrauterine and postnatal undernutrition on normal brain development." _Annals of the New York Academy of Sciences_, 205, 1973, pp. 231-244.

Chase, H. P. and H. P. Martin. "Undernutrition and child development." _New England Journal of Medicine_, 282, 1970, pp. 933-939.

Cheyne, W. M. and G. Jahoda. "Emotional sensitivity and intelligence in children from orphanages and normal homes." _Journal of Child Psychology and Psychiatry_, 12, 1971, pp. 77-90.

Davids, A., R. H. Halden, and G. B. Gray. "Maternal anxiety during pregnancy and adequacy of mother and child adjustment eight months following childbirth." _Child Development_, 34, 1963, pp. 993-1002.

De Hirsch, K., J. Jansky, and W. S. Langford. "Comparisons between prematurely and maturely born children at three age levels." _American Journal of Orthopsychiatry_, 36, 1966, pp. 616-628.

Drillien, C. M. and E. M. Wilkinson. "Emotional stress and mongoloid births." _Developmental Medicine and Child Neurology_, 6, 1964, pp. 140-143.

Elmer, E. and G. S. Gregg. "Developmental characteristics of abused children." _Pediatrics_, 40, 1967, pp. 596-602.

Gavrin, J. B. and L. S. Sacks. "Growth potential of preschool-aged child in institutional care: a positive approach to a negative condition." _American Journal of Orthopsychiatry_, 33, 1963, pp. 399-408.

Hansen, A. B. "Short term differences of infant development in nursery homes and in private families." _Acta Paediatrica Scandinavica_, 60, 1971, pp. 571-577.

Hansen, J. D. L., C. Freesemann, A. D. Moodie, and E. D. Evans. "What does nutritional growth retardation imply?" _Pediatrics_, 47, 1971, pp. 299-311.

Heilbrun, H. "Maternal child rearing and creativity in sons." Journal of
    Genetic Psychology, 119, 1971, pp. 175-179.

Klatskin, E. H., M. E. McGarry, and M. S. Steward. "Variability in developmen-
    tal test patterns as a sequel of neonatal stress." Child Development,
    37, 1966, pp. 819-826.

Klein, R. E. et al. "Is big smart? The relation of growth to cognition."
    Journal of Health and Social Behavior, 13, 1972, pp. 219-225.

Landy, F., B. G. Rosenberg, and B. Sutton-Smith. "The effect of limited father
    absence on cognitive development." Child Development, 40, 1969, pp.
    941-944.

Lubchenco, L. O., M. Delivoria-Papadopoulos, and D. Searls. "Long-term follow-
    up studies of prematurely born infants. II. Influence of birth weight
    and gestational age on sequelae." Journal of Pediatrics, 80, 1972, pp.
    509-512.

Meierhofer, M. "Institutional care of children." Royal Society of Health
    Journal, 93, 1973, pp. 29-30.

Morse, C. W., O. J. Sahler, and S. B. Friedman. "A three-year follow-up study
    of abused and neglected children." American Journal of Diseases of Chil-
    dren, 120, 1970, pp. 439-446.

Pollitt, E. "Behavioral correlates of severe malnutrition in man." in W. M.
    Moore, M. M. Silverberg and M. S. Read, eds., Nutrition, Growth and De-
    velopment of North American Indian Children. DHEW Publication No. (NIH)
    72-26, 1972, pp. 151-166.

Pollitt, E. "Behavior of infant in causation of nutritional marasmus." The
    American Journal of Clinical Nutrition, 26, 1973, pp. 264-270.

Richardson, S. A. "Ecology of malnutrition: nonnutritional factors influenc-
    ing intellectual and behavioral development." in Nutrition, the Nervous
    System, and Behavior. Pan American Health Organization, Scientific Pub-
    lication No. 251, 1974.

Richardson, S. A., H. G. Birch, and M. E. Hertzig. "School performance of chil-
    dren who were severely malnourished in infancy." American Journal of
    Mental Deficiency, 77, 1973, pp. 623-632.

Robinson, N. M. and H. B. Robinson. "A follow-up study of children of low birth
    weight and control children at school age." Pediatrics, 35, 1965, pp.
    425-433.

Saltz, R. "Effects of part-time mothering on I.Q. and S.Q. of young institu-
    tionalized children." Child Development, 44, 1973, pp. 166-170.

Scarr-Salapatek, S. and M. L. Williams. "The effects of early stimulation on
    low-birth weight infants." Child Development, 44, 1973, pp. 94-101.

Shipe, D. and A. M. Shotwell. "Effect of out-of-home care on mongoloid chil-
    dren: a continuation study." American Journal of Mental Deficiency, 69,
    1965, pp. 649-652.

Srikantia, S. G. and C. Y. Sastri. "Observations on malnutrition and mental development." Indian Journal of Mental Research, 59, (Suppl.), 1971, pp. 216-220.

Stedman, D. J. and D. H. Eichorn. "A comparison of the growth and development of institutionalized and home-reared mongoloids during infancy and early childhood." American Journal of Mental Deficiency, 69, 1964, pp. 391-401.

Stein, Z., M. Susser, G. Saenger, and F. Marolla. "Nutrition and mental performance." Science, 178, 1972, pp. 708-713.

Sutton-Smith, B., B. G. Rosenberg, and F. Landy. "Father-absence effects in families of different sibling compositions." Child Development, 39, 1968, pp. 1213-1221.

Taylor, A. "Follow-up of institutionalized infants' concept formation ability at age 12." American Journal of Orthopsychiatry, 40, 1970, pp. 441-447.

Werner, E. E., M. P. Honzik, and R. S. Smith. "Prediction of intelligence and achievement at ten years from twenty months pediatric and psychologic examinations." Child Development, 39, 1968, pp. 1063-1075.

Wiener, G. "The relationship of birth weight and length of gestation to intellectual development at ages 8-10 years." Journal of Pediatrics, 76, 1970, pp. 694-699.

Wiener, G., R. V. Rider, W. C. Oppel, L. K. Fischer, and P. A. Harper. "Psychological correlates of low birth weight at six to seven years of age." Pediatrics, 35, 1965, pp. 434-442.

Willerman, L. and J. A. Churchill. "Intelligence and birth weight in identical twins." Child Development, 38, 1967, pp. 623-629.

Willerman, L. and R. E. Stafford. "Maternal effects on intellectual functioning." Behavior Genetics, 2, 1972, pp. 321-325.

Yarrow, L. J. "Research in dimensions of early maternal care." Merrill-Palmer Quarterly, 9, 1963, pp. 101-114.

CHAPTER 6

SOCIAL-EMOTIONAL DEVELOPMENT

The nature of the subject in this section does not lend itself to the kind of organization found in the material on physical and cognitive development. In fact, the very title "Social-Emotional Development" is an arbitrary choice. This section could as well be entitled "personality development," "character development," "socialization," or "psychological development," depending on the particular theoretical perspective taken. This inquiry into "emotional" abuse and neglect of children investigates caretaking and environmental factors as these are reflected in behavioral patterns and affective states, but are not necessarily reflected in the physical or cognitive condition of the subjects.

In the previous discussion of physical and mental development, the material was organized around common "dependent" variables. It is not possible to organize social-emotional development in this manner for three reasons. First, the plethora of variables studied preclude any logical grouping of the data. Second, the phenomena under consideration do not lend themselves to the same kinds of operational definitions and measures. Low birth weight, head circumference, growth rates, and the like are quantifiable; even intelligence, the validity of the measurement notwithstanding, has specifiable performance referents. The variables under study here are not of that nature. Many are observable behaviors that can be measured quantitatively, while others are only based on inference from observable behavior reflecting internal affective states.

The most difficult problem in grouping studies in terms of what is "harmful" to children is that many of the variables under study can be judged harmful or beneficial only within the context of social values. For instance, the issue of what degree of aggression or dependence is positive or negative in children's development ultimately rests on how aggressive or dependent a society wants its members to be. The issue of harm really involves the issues of social desirability and undesirability, and the level of consensus is far lower than is the agreement with respect to physical growth and cognitive development. It is safer to assume that a consensus exists in desiring children to be as big, strong, and smart as they can be, than to assume such consensus about what constitutes good behavior.

In this section we have abandoned, for the most part, our groupings of studies by dependent variables or by risks to children. Instead, the studies have been grouped by what we believe to be the major pre-occupations in the field, a field that can broadly be described as inquiry into the relationship between parental behavior and child behavior. The major portion of work has been devoted to maternal or mothering behavior and has focused on babies and very young children. We discuss first studies that deal with mother-child interaction as a unitary phenomenon, rather than as an interaction where maternal behavior is treated as antecedent to the child's. Next, we look at studies of early infant functioning and emphasize factors present in the neonate, rather than in the environment, that are thought to influence behavior. This is followed by a discussion of early childhood attachment and separation behavior. We have also included a review of studies that are concerned with risks to children, mental illness, and behavior disorders. These studies deal with children already identified as "ill" or "disordered" and seek an etiologic link to parental behavior; all are retrospective and ex post facto. It is necessary to make this point because the relative certainty that underlies much of the work in early infant functioning simply is not possible in this kind of work. Strong correlations between specifiable maternal behaviors and infant responses such as crying cannot be interpreted as producing phenomena such as mental illness or delinquency.

Mother-Child Interaction

Because the mother has the socially prescribed role of primary caretaker of her infant, it is assumed that she is the individual most responsible for the infant's survival and well-being. Consequently, this mother-infant dyad has been the principal focus of child development research. In some cases the father or another person may take the primary caretaking role, but these cases are considered exceptions and do not dispel the theory that the infant first forms a close social relationship with the mother.

Even though studies lack agreement on which specific factors are most important in early development, there is "overwhelming theoretical consensus that the most significant influence in the early environment is the infant's relationship with its mother" (Yarrow, 1963). Because much early learning is based on maternal reinforcement and early imitation of maternal behaviors, the effects of the interaction between a mother and her infant may be far-reaching. Indeed, the continuing relationship between the mother and her growing child may be a significant factor in that child's overall development.

In this discussion, the mother-child interaction is considered the dependent variable or the intervening variable. Factors affecting mother-child interaction and their effects on the child are also included in the study.

Repeated reference is made throughout this literature to the possible deleterious effects of disorders in mother-child interaction. A few of the childhood problems that have been associated with such disorders include anorexia (Di Cagno and Ravetto, 1968), feeding problems (Brandon, 1970), learning problems (Brodie and Winterbottom, 1967), lower intelligence (Dandes and Dow, 1969), hypotonia (Buda, Rothney, and Rabe, 1972), aggression (McCord, McCord, and Howard, 1963), and psychiatric problems (Rousell and Edwards, 1971). These and other negative effects on children have been identified in investigations that utilized the mother-child interaction as the independent variable. The evidence of such effects gives support to the notion that a deficient mother-child interaction must be considered a category of risk in any discussion of child development.

A number of methodological issues should be clarified prior to our discussion. Studies on mother-child interaction have usually examined only a limited number of variables in maternal care and have tended to focus only on the child's behavior. We have tried to avoid both of these limitations by concentrating instead on the interaction between maternal and child behaviors. Only those studies that deal with such an interaction are examined.

Secondly, it must be noted that the studies we cite have used a broad range of methods, and some have even failed to include "normal" mother-child interactive behavior within their samples. Examples of this deficiency are studies that make use of questionnaires or interviews and retrospective studies that rely on verbal reports. By and large, observation studies are more valid, but when they are too highly structured or take place in a laboratory setting, they also are susceptible to bias and error. An excellent review of this methodology employed by observation studies of parent-child interaction was published by Lytton (1971). He noted that a major dilemma facing such studies is to determine the kinds of data distortions they are willing to tolerate and how to minimize their effect. Investigations tend to differ totally on their control of stimuli, recording of behaviors, the conceptualization of summary variables, and the range and type of behavior sampled. There is generally little agreement as to which maternal or child characteristics are important to consider. Another problem encountered in the research on child development is agreement on identification of specific child and maternal needs met in the mother-child interaction. Terms such as "nurturant," "healthy," "warm," and "accepting" are commonly used, but these concepts lack operational definitions. Despite these methodological problems, the view of mother-child interaction as a dependent variable helps to clarify some of the issues involved in explaining the linkages among factors that ultimately place children at risk of deleterious effects.

Mother-Child Interaction as a Circular Process

Several theorists have proposed that mother-child interaction is a circular process that lacks any specific point at which cause-and-effect relationships might be determined. Each behavior or response by one member of the mother-child dyad elicits some behavior by the other member that, in turn, elicits a behavior by the former. Because the methodology of relevant studies is frequently correlational in nature, only associations between maternal and child behaviors can be identified. Disorders of mother-child interaction are generally viewed as the presence of behaviors by one member of the mother-child dyad that are associated with problem behaviors on the part of the other member. Such disorders are often composed of associations between problem behaviors exhibited by both the mother and the child.

Yarrow (1963) correlated behavior and IQ ratings of 40 six-month-old babies with assessments of the mother's interaction with the infant in the areas of need-gratification and tension reduction, provision of stimulation, and affectional-emotional interchange. His results showed that most of the maternal variables were highly correlated with developmental progress and other characteristics of the infant. The highest correlations were found between IQ and the amount and quality of stimulation provided by the mother, between the infant's response to stress and the maternal behaviors of sensitivity, adaptation, involvement, and acceptance. There were lower correlations between infant characteristics and both the consistency and exclusiveness of maternal behaviors, suggesting a minimal level of consistency at this age with other factors such as contact. The investigator pointed out that with data on early interactions it is extremely difficult to specify antecedent conditions.

Di Cagno and Ravetto (1968), in their study of 30 children who had a history of clearly non-organic anorexia in the first year of life and an abnormal personality structure later in life, described two different forms of circular patterns in mother-child interaction. In the neurotic form, maternal personality dysfunctions (e.g., anxiety, depression, insecurity) elicited defensive responses in the child (e.g., not eating) that, in turn, strengthened the anxiety or depression of the mother. In the psychotic form, the aggressive, obsessive tendencies of the mother, creating a persistent non-acceptance relationship towards the child, were met with aggression by the child in the form of a refusal to introject the maternal object that, in turn, elicited more aggression on the part of the mother. The investigators noted that both forms of mother-child interaction consisted of irrepressible circular processes arising from the echo-effect that the frustrating behavior of each member had on the other.

In a longitudinal study, Bennett (1971) observed ten infants twice a week for the first month of life, paying particular attention to the kinds of responses the infant evoked in the caretaker. The early infant characteristics (e.g., alertness, visual behavior, activity, and facial movements) were interpreted by the caretaker as affect and approach responses, thus resulting in the construction of a fantasy about the infant's "personality." The fantasies not only shaped the attitude and behavior of the caretaker, but also influenced changes in infant behavior.

Other methods have been used in an effort to determine the directional influence of multiple variables. Stern et al. (1969) used a factor analytic method on a matrix of intercorrelations between maternal characteristics and infant characteristics appearing at particular developmental periods. Ratings of a sample of 30 mothers and children at the age of one year yielded nine factors. The loading patterns suggested a causal relationship between the personality characteristics of the mother, the mode of maternal behavior she adopted, and the responses and development of her infant. The nine factors appeared to be distributed along a continuum ranging from child-centered to mother-centered maternal functioning, a continuum that appeared to be related to psychopathy in both mother and child as the degree of maternal self-reference increased.

Prenatal Factors

Such conceptual issues as the direction of influence have been the concern of several theorists, but many remain interested in descriptive analyses of mother-child interaction using comparative designs to assess the influence of other variables on mother-child interaction.

A few studies have tried to assess the impact of prenatal factors on later mother-infant interaction. In a longitudinal study by Davids, Halden, and Gray (1963) 50 pregnant women were dichotomized on the basis of a battery of psychological tests into a "high anxiety" group and a "low anxiety" group. Both groups of mothers were seen with their children for a psychological assessment eight months following childbirth. Mothers who were highly anxious during pregnancy had negative child-rearing attitudes and received less favorable ratings on the basis of an observation of the mother-child interaction at the time of the eight month assessment. The children of the "low anxiety" mothers received significantly higher developmental quotients on the Bayley Infant Mental and Motor Scales. The investigators pointed out that the findings were consistent with the prediction that women who are highly anxious during pregnancy often have negative parental attitudes during their child's early development. These children also fare less well on tests of intellectual development and indices of emotional adjustment. In review of emotional factors in the prenatal environment, Ferreira (1965) cited a number of empirical studies showing that maternal stress during pregnancy is correlated with later infant problem behavior and with negative maternal emotional attitudes during the child's development. Since such studies usually fail to control for possible postnatal influences, their conclusions must be considered tenuous.

Socioeconomic Differences

The demographic factor of socioeconomic status has been examined by Kogan and Wimberger (1971). On the basis of laboratory observations of mother-child interaction, they compared ten mother-child pairs of lower SES with ten mother-child pairs of middle SES, paying particular attention to the interactive behavioral patterns of relative status, affection, and involvement. Their results showed that the "culturally deprived" mothers and children responded to each other with as much affection as the "culturally advantaged" dyads. The lower SES pairs, however, were more detached from each other: they engaged in less social interchange; the children's behavior was less likely to be similar to their mother's; and their patterns of behavior were more likely to be based on status contingencies. The low SES mothers disagreed with their children more, were less helpful, gave more unfriendly orders, and engaged in less nonverbal communication. The children were more likely to voice their opinions and to do so in a strident manner. Overall, "disadvantaged" mother-child pairs were less actively engaged in interaction than were the "culturally advantaged" mother-child pairs.

Using questionnaire responses, Rosen (1964) correlated the value preferences of 122 boys, aged eight to fourteen years, with the values of their mothers. He found that value similarity was related to social class, with middle-class families having greater similarity in values than lower-class families.

In addition, independence training and methods of discipline, two important areas of childrearing, were found to be related to value transmission. Mothers whose values were shared by their sons were found to engage more in early independence training and to resort more often to "love-oriented" techniques of discipline, such as display of affection, reasoning, and appeal to standards, than were mothers whose sons tended not to share their values. The data revealed that middle-class parents trained their children earlier, were more affectionate, and employed "conditional-love" techniques of discipline to a greater extent than did lower-class parents.

Another study that supported these conclusions focused first on the sex of the child as a variable, then compared its results with other studies to examine social class differences. Using laboratory observation techniques with 17 precoded behavior categories, Walters, Connor, and Zunich (1964) examined the facility and inhibitory behaviors of 40 lower-class mothers in interaction with their three to five-year-old children, 20 of whom were boys and 20 of whom were girls. Although most of the behavior frequencies were independent of the sex of the child, mother-daughter interaction involved more contact, whereas mothers with sons evidenced more restrictive behavior. Comparing these findings with those of a study of middle- and upper-class mothers and their children, the investigators found that the lower-class mothers spent significantly more time than did middle- and upper-class mothers as silent onlookers, uninvolved with the children, and engaged in significantly less directing, helping, structuring, and teaching behaviors.

In a correlational study, Tulkin and Cohler (1973) examined childrearing attitudes and the manner in which 56 white mothers of diverse economic backgrounds related to their young children. They observed mother-child interaction in the home setting and they obtained data on childrearing attitudes through the use of a multi-variate attitude scale. They then segregated data by SES. Correlational analysis revealed class-related attitudinal differences. The attitudes of middle-class mothers reflected more moderate control of aggressive impulses, greater encouragement of reciprocity, greater acceptance of emotional complexities involved in childrearing, and greater comfort in perceiving and meeting the young child's physical needs than did those of working-class mothers. The investigators suggested that the major differences between the two SES groups may be due to differences in the mothers' perceptions of their roles in their children's development. Working-class mothers often felt they had little influence over the development of their children.

Even though the evidence supports the existence of differences in mother-child interaction based on socioeconomic status, such studies should be considered inconclusive due to their lack of homogeneity, especially their lack of internal controls. The interpretation given to these differences in relation to their benign or deleterious effects on the children poses another problem. There is always a tendency to attribute "good" effects to middle-class behavior and "bad" effects to lower-class behavior. But if one allows for the different expectations for children from different social strata, it is quite conceivable that successful adaptation might well require the development of different characteristics for children from each social stratum.

Family Size and Density

Maternal availability is another demographic variable investigated in descriptive studies on mother-child interaction. The relevant studies are those examining the effects of family size and density and the exclusiveness of caretaking. Waldrop and Bell (1964) correlated an index of family size and density based on four pertinent components, with a measure of the preschool dependency behavior of 44 preschool boys as rated on the scale "Child initiated contact with female nursery school teacher." They obtained a correlation of .53, suggesting that males from large congested families initiated contact more frequently. The investigators postulated that family density could affect a mother's contact behavior with a child and her ability to prevent the occurrence of anxiety-producing situations, regardless of her method of childrearing. The measurement of maternal availability, based on a family size and density index, was supported by findings showing a negative relation between the index and the measure of maternal contact made in the home. That is, the mother-child interaction may suffer because of the demands placed on the mother by the competing needs of the other children.

In another study, Waldrop and Bell (1966) observed 74 infants at about 80 hours of age and followed up 55 of them at two and a half years of age to investigate the relationship between newborn behavior and family size and density. The infants born to the mothers who had experienced a large number of closely-spaced pregnancies were found to be more lethargic and later more dependent than infants born to mothers who had experienced fewer pregnancies that were more widely spaced. Again, the investigators emphasized the probability of decreased maternal availability in large, dense families.

In his study of SES differences in value transmission between mothers and their sons, Rosen (1964) also found that at all class levels, small and medium-sized families had higher levels of value similarity than did large families. If family size and density can be interpreted as indicators of maternal availability, it appears that this factor can set differential conditions for mother-child interaction with resulting qualitative differences in the interaction.

In a different approach, Caldwell et al. (1963) examined the influence of intense available maternal contact with a longitudinal study of caretaker exclusiveness. Patterns of mother-infant interaction in families where mothering was provided by only one person (monomatric) were compared with those of families where mothering was provided by more than one person (polymatric). Interviews and observations of 37 mothers and their one-year-old infants rated infants from monomatric families as more active, more emotionally dependent on their mothers, and more emotional in their interactions with their mothers. Their mothers, in turn, were more emotionally dependent on the infants, more solicitous about their infants' welfare, more playful, and more tolerant of irritating behavior. The investigators postulated that in polymatric families, characterized by the availability of less intense maternal contact, unresolved dependency needs interfere with the establishment of a close mother-infant affectional bond. That is, maternal availability as indicated by caretaker exclusiveness may be an important factor in determining the quality of mother-child interaction.

Special Characteristics of Children

Two studies by Kogan have attempted to describe the mother-child interaction in families of handicapped or disturbed children. Using laboratory observational methods, Kogan and Wimberger (1971) compared the interaction patterns between ten disturbed children and their mothers with those of ten normal children. They reported a more frequent occurrence of strongly controlling behaviors on the part of the mothers of disturbed children. These mothers tended to exercise their control by telling their children what to do; mothers of normal children tended to exercise their control not by directing their behavior, but by expressing their disapproval or acceptance of what the children had already done.

Similar observational techniques involving both verbal and non-verbal behavior were used by Kogan and Tyler (1973) to analyze the mother-child interactions of ten physically handicapped children, six mentally retarded children, and 15 non-handicapped children and their mothers. Mothers of physically handicapped children showed more assertive control and warmth than did both mothers of non-handicapped children and mothers of mentally retarded children. The physically handicapped children interacted at a lower involvement level than did the non-handicapped children, but they displayed more assertive controlling behavior than did the mentally retarded children.

Summary

Thus far, we have reviewed work that treats mother-child interaction as a unitary phenomenon -- an interactive process that can be affected by factors external to both mother and child. Although the specific variables examined were multiple and diverse, precluding summary statements across studies, certain common themes exist. These studies indicate that it may well be invalid to search for explanations of the quality of mother-child interaction solely in factors resident in the mother, such as her own personality characteristics. Certainly the research relating to socioeconomic status and to family size and density suggests that external situational factors can contribute to mother-child interaction.

In the next part of our discussion, studies that deal with early infant functioning are more closely investigated. These studies examine what the infant, rather than just the mother, brings to the mother-child interaction. We find that individual differences at birth in infants are directly related to mother-child interaction.

Early Infant Functioning

Development in the human infant has received increasing attention in the past decade as the theory of pre-set biological programming has given way to a more social-environmental orientation in infant development. Experts in the field now generally believe that infants are receptive and vulnerable to external influences as they interact with people and forces in the environment. This interaction has a major impact on the child's development.

Some of the research on infant development, however, has suggested certain innate individual differences at birth. Nisbett and Gurwitz (1970) conducted an experimental study of the eating behavior of newborns and found that heavier birth weight is associated with obesity in later life. When newborn infants were given sweetened formula, heavier infants would increase their intake significantly. When sucking was made more difficult, heavy infants were less willing to exert effort to obtain food. Female infants were more responsive to the sweet taste and less willing to work for their formulas than their male counterparts. These researchers found parallel weight and sex differences in human adults and suggested that individual differences in eating behavior among humans at birth are an innate characteristic.

Anneliese Korner (1971), in a discussion on differences in infants at birth and in later development, stated that there are individual differences in irritability among infants that have an impact on the infant-caretaker interaction: the response the infant elicits from the caretaker depends on the infant as well as the caretaker. The infant's capacity for and style of response to soothing influence the caretaker's perception of his/her competence. Babies also differ in the intensity of their oral drives and their capacity for self-comforting and therefore require different degrees of mediating, tension-reducing behavior from the caretaker. These different oral demands may also determine or influence the intensity of the weaning period.

Lewis et al. (1967) have shown that individual infant endowments contribute to subsequent development. For example, they observed through the use of the Apgar Scale that children who rated lower on the scale were significantly less attentive than were those infants who rated higher. The authors suggest that the development of a finer differentiation within the Apgar Scale may have diagnostic value in predicting subsequent development.

The effects of certain caretaker behaviors, however, in conjunction with innate character differences in infants, now present investigators with the opportunity to study the interaction among an array of relevant variables. Some of this work has sought to establish relationships between differences in infant behavior, especially feeding behavior, and differences with caretaker behavior.

In a ten-day study of 38 infants, some of whom were bottle-fed and others of whom were breast-fed, Bernal (1972) observed differences in infant feeding behavior. He cites studies that attribute the higher weight gain and obesity prevalent among bottle-fed babies to the higher protein content in the milk. Some of these studies also assign a higher risk of illness to bottle-fed babies. These results should be interpreted with caution because they do not include the contextual complexity of each infant's socioeconomic environment, which affects the infant's feeding behavior. For example, the influence of variables such as privacy, modesty, family environment, and family size, make it difficult to confirm clearly a direct associative relationship between feeding method and feeding behavior.

Thoman, Barnett, and Leiderman (1971) investigated differences in infant feeding behavior during the first 12 hours of life and found that infants of primiparous mothers were fed more frequently than were those fed by nurses. The nurse-fed infants required less time with fewer intervals and consumed more formula. They concluded that the mother's feeding pattern and behavior during feeding may obscure or even preclude expression of the infant's congenital response tendencies.

Bennett (1971) undertook an observational, longitudinal study of infant-nurse interaction during the first few weeks of life for ten infants. He found that the way the caretaker, in this case the nurse, perceived the infant's behavior was reflected in her spontaneous behavior and response to the infant and vice-versa: the infant developed a style of response and temperament based upon cues from the caretaker, such as eye movement, mouth movement, and overall facial expression.

Other studies have examined the commonalities among infant responses to different kinds of caretaking behaviors. Korner and Thoman (1972) in their research on 40 two-year-old children who had been healthy, full-term newborns replicated common maternal soothing techniques and associated these with crying time during and after intervention. Certain types of interventions were more effective than others. For example, vestibular stimulation was more effective than contact without moving the infant. They found, in addition, that the mode of feeding was not related to effective soothing techniques. Korner and Thoman drew the conclusion that the soothing effects, which have been attributed solely to contact comfort, may be largely a function of vestibular-proprioceptive stimulation that accompanies most contact between mother and child.

Evidence of the importance of the earliest days of life in establishing expectations for key environmental features is given in a study by Burns et al. (1972). Twenty-seven normal infants were divided into three groups from birth through 56 days, with various combinations of caretaker and rooming-in arrangements for each group. Feeding habits and distress in feeding were correlated with the different caretaker environments. Those children with multiple caretakers and fixed feeding schedules in the newborn nursery registered high distress scores. When the baby shifted to a single caretaker rooming-in, this high level was reduced approximately to that of the normative comparison.

While innate differences may characterize newborns, the relative persistence of effects of these characteristics in subsequent development has been questioned. Bell and Ainsworth (1972) concluded that, by the end of the first year, the individual differences in children's crying behavior are more a reflection of maternal responsiveness than of differences in infant irritability. They found that the promptness of response, rather than just the quality of response, by the mother was the most effective in reducing crying. This rapid responsiveness encouraged non-crying modes of communication by the infant and decreased the amount of crying as well.

These findings are supported by Bernal's study (1972) of 77 mother-infant pairs during the first ten days of the infant's life. If a second child, the baby showed a lower crying score due to a more rapid response and more frequent feeding by the mother than did children who were first born. Success in breast-feeding also made those mothers more open to flexible feeding schedules.

In addition to research on innate differences, other work has sought to identify the effects of prenatal and birth conditions on newborn behavior, apart from caretaker behavior. Several studies have pointed out possible maternal and environmental factors that are associated with newborn behavior. In an experimental study, Standley et al. (1974) examined the possible effects of local-regional anesthetics and analgesics administered during childbirth on behavioral characteristics of infants at two to three days of age. Sixty first-born healthy infants between 58 and 72 hours of age were evaluated on the Brazelton neo-natal assessment scale. The results showed that the administration of local-regional anesthesia was correlated significantly with decreased motor maturity and greater irritability. Jerky movements in small arcs, startles, tremulous motions, frequent state changes, and crying were more common in babies born of anesthetized mothers. Analgesia usage was also significantly related to lower scores on motor maturity.

Ottinger and Simmons (1964) compared the behavior of one- to four-day-old neonates of ten mothers who had scored high on the IPAT Anxiety Scale during pregnancy to the neonates of nine mothers who had scored low on the IPAT. The babies of the two groups did not differ in birth weight or weight during the first four days of life, but the babies' crying behavior was directly and significantly related to the mothers' anxiety level during pregnancy. Since this difference in crying behavior was present before but not after feeding, the investigators concluded that it was a prenatal and/or genetic phenomenon rather than a function of differences in maternal handling during feeding.

Waldrop and Bell (1966) observed the behavior of 74 infants at the age of three days and later at two and a half years to investigate the relationship between newborn behavioral characteristics and several indices of family size and density. Overall, a distinctive newborn behavior pattern was found in infants born into large, dense families, and this pattern was related significantly to later dependency behavior. At the age of three days, infants born to the mothers who had experienced a large number of closely spaced pregnancies were low in sucking rate, cried less when sucking was interrupted, and were more lethargic than were infants born to mothers who had experienced fewer and more widely spaced pregnancies.

In conclusion, studies of early infant functioning clearly indicate that babies interact with their environment and are not simply passive receptors absorbing its impact. The relationship of constitutional factors with caretaking behavior is far from being fully understood, and, like many other issues in early infant functioning, it is an area of research that is being explored by more investigators who are evolving methodological tools to encompass more variables.

Attachment, Exploration, and Separation Anxiety

Looking at mother-child interaction provides one perspective on child development, but this interaction is related to the more specific behavior characteristics of attachment, exploration, and separation anxiety. The difficulty in examining this area is that, while the definitional terms encompass behavior in operational terms, the affective aspect of behavior is excluded. Provence (1975) found the term "attachment behavior" unsatisfying in her work because it is wrongly equated with "relationship," which she considers conceptually and theoretically different. As she pointed out in an interview:

> We talk about children forming attachments and forming relationships; then we gain evidence for that by observing the interactions between the child and parent in front of other people and draw inferences from that. I find the term "attachment behavior" unsatisfying. There is a danger of equating that with "relationship;" they partake of each other, but they aren't conceptually or theoretically the same. Unless you are sympathetic to a more complicated theory of the mental life of the child, you can be deceived by superficial behavior that would suggest that the child is strongly or weakly attached, so it isn't very useful clinically.

Separation is another related area that has already gained particular attention in the study of neglect and abuse. Since attachment is so important, harm is expected to come to children from premature breaking of such an attachment. But children can also be harmed by not developing independence. Specifying harm in this sense involves the difficult task of distinguishing between healthy attachment and over-attachment. Such decisions call for qualitative judgments about kinds of attachments that preclude an easy transition through the developmental task of establishing independence.

Robert Sears (1975) considered the variables of separation and attachment insufficiently differentiated to allow a valid test of independent variables on the child's behavior in a separation and attachment situation. In an interview, he elaborated:

> Attachment was a very useful first approximation to cir-
> cumscribe an area of interaction between parents and
> children. But now we are getting to the point where we
> can break it down further, and we may just have to throw
> out "attachment" and start talking about a whole dimen-
> sion of the "positive love relationship" and the "posi-
> tive hate relationship." Part of the developmental task
> of the child is learning how to reduce the attachment or
> how to get along without the "positive love relationship."
> Descriptively, we have a rough notion as to what happens.
> Theoretically, we know very little about the qualities in
> the children or the influences on the children that make
> it easy or difficult for them to separate from the parents.

There is, then, a consensus that "attachment" -- the establishment of a primary nuclear relationship -- is of over-riding importance in all aspects of a child's development. Given the state of knowledge, however, the more precise kinds of information necessary to answer questions regarding harm to children (e.g., what kinds of harm, with what kinds of lasting effects) are not available. Issues are extant at the theoretical and conceptual level and hence in the in-terpretation of the research findings that do exist.

Operational definitions cover a broad range of experiences depending on the investigator and the nature of the study. Ainsworth and Bell (1970), who have done extensive research on attachment behavior, regard it as an affectual bond that a person forms with another person, a tie that binds them in space and endures over time. They define attachment behavior as that which promotes prox-imity or contact, such as approaching, following, lingering, smiling, crying, and calling. Van Leewen and Tuma (1972) define attachment behavior as movement toward the mother and exploratory behavior as movement away from the mother to-ward the environment. In another study, Rubenstein (1967) observed children's tactile and oral responses to a single novel stimulus presented to them for ten minutes and compared these responses to reactions to a familiar stimulus. He then developed an exploratory behavior index based in part on these responses.

Attachment behavior in ten-month-old infants was found to be significant-ly related to social class among middle and working-class infants (Tulkin and Cohler, 1973). When the infants of working mothers and unemployed mothers were compared, initial findings were that working mothers' infants cried less frequently and crawled less frequently to the mother upon her return. But, in further analysis of the data, Tulkin and Cohler concluded that no single index of attachment can serve as a basis for judging whether an infant has become attached and that separation distress may not be a valid indication of attachment.

Ainsworth (1964) studied attachment and separation behavior in 28 African infants ranging in age from two to 15 months. He identified 13 behavior patterns between infant and mother and other favorite figures, omitting behavior associated solely with feeding. The author found that attachments are largely dependent on the infant's own initiative; infants become attached through their own activity, rather than through stimulation or passive satisfaction of their creature comfort needs. Furthermore, attachment patterns do not necessarily depend upon physical contact. Attachment can be transferred to other figures when infants have the opportunity to interact with people other than their mothers. The interaction between the infant and the mother is viewed as a chain of behaviors initiated either by the mother or by the infant to which the other responds. The author hypothesizes that maternal deprivation is best defined as insufficient interaction between the infant and a mother figure, not merely as a lack of stimulation. Maternal deprivation results from the lack of adult response to the behavior infants initiate, including their attachment behavior.

Supporting this perspective is a comparative study by Rubenstein (1967) that examines maternal attentiveness and relates it to exploratory behavior in the infant. He found a positive relationship between a quantified measure of sensory-social stimulation and the infant's exploratory behavior. While the individual infant's needs for stimulation differed, the infants who failed to receive varied stimulation were less responsive to novelty than were infants accustomed to a high degree of varied experiences. The latter group exhibited less exploratory behavior, as defined in this study. Repetitive, unvarying stimulation did not facilitate exploration and the author suggests that the variety inherent in large quantities of attentiveness is the critical factor in generating exploratory behavior. Stimulation of institutionalized infants may be an important factor in preventing the apathy that maternal separation sometimes initiates.

Several authors have concluded that exploratory behavior is related to the mother's presence and absolute proximity (Ainsworth and Bell, 1970; Ricciuti, 1964; Morgan and Ricciuti, 1969). In an experimental study, Ainsworth and Bell (1970) observed the behavior of 56 white, middle-class infants 49 to 51 weeks old in reaction to a strange environment. The mother's presence was found to encourage exploratory behavior; her absence depressed exploration and heightened attachment behavior. During separation, crying and search behavior increased. Reunion between mother and infant resulted in active contact-maintaining behavior and close proximity. These authors suggest that the definitions of attachment and attachment behavior should be broad enough to include the following points: (1) Attachment is not coincident with attachment behavior. While the latter may be heightened or diminished by conditions that can be specified empirically, the former cannot; (2) Attachment behavior is heightened in a situation perceived as threatening; (3) Although the state of being attached and the presence of the attachment object may support and facilitate exploratory behaviors, heavy attachment behavior is incompatible with exploratory behavior; and (4) Although attachment behavior may diminish or disappear in certain conditions, the actual attachment is not necessarily diminished.

Van Leewen and Tuma (1972) verified Ainsworth's concepts in their longitudinal study of 16 nursery school children ranging in age from two years, 11 months to four years, three months. All the children showed distress upon entering nursery school, as evidenced by their withdrawal and decrease in exploratory behavior. The younger children entering nursery school were less attached and more exploratory, but showed consistently and significantly increased attachment by the fifteenth day of school. They needed free access to the mother. In contrast, the older children maintained their attachment level. This difference in attachment behavior and the general negative reaction to entering nursery school are not necessarily due to pathology of the child or to faulty care in the nursery school. They are appropriate reactions, for that age, to prolonged and repeated separation, although these normal reactions can be aggravated by inadequate environmental conditions and unresponsiveness to attachment needs.

Tennes and Lampl (1964) studied stranger and separation anxiety in infants three to 23 months old, measuring on a six point scale the intensity, immediacy, duration, and ease of anxiety reduction. The responses were recorded by two independent judges. They related their results to Benjamin's theory of anxiety and development: infants who exhibited fear responses to strangers showed higher levels of anxiety later on than did infants who did not have fearful responses to strangers. Separation anxiety was also strongly linked to later stranger anxiety.

From the studies cited, we conclude that attachment behavior, exploratory behavior, separation, and stranger anxiety are interactive and related. As the intensity of attachment feelings change, children increase their exploratory behavior in response to environmental stimuli. As this occurs, and perhaps even in response to this developmental change, interactions with the caretaker can impede or enhance the shift from attachment to exploratory behavior. The character of the bond that has been established between caretaker and infant, which is as much a function of the infant's endowments as of the caretaker's behavior, determines the duration and depth of these childhood stages of development. It must be noted, however, that the events and environment prior and subsequent to birth also shape the responses and character of the infant. Environmental influences may even serve to establish patterns that endure throughout the life of the individual.

By focusing almost exclusively on attachment behavior, child development specialists have failed to consider the functional and adaptive importance of detachment behavior. From the moment of birth, infants experience conflicting desires, based upon biological and physiological determinants, for proximity to caretakers and, at the same time, distance from them. This attachment-detachment process is continuous throughout development.

Again, a cautionary note must be sounded regarding the meaning of attachment behavior. Some researchers hesitate to equate attachment behavior with the deep affective state whose development the behavior is assumed to signal. Given this state of affairs, the meaning of "maternal deprivation" must also be treated cautiously, particularly when viewed as an etiologic agent of childhood and adult disturbances. Certainly there is nothing in these studies that would permit the equation of "maternal deprivation" meaning no maternal figure at all with "maternal deprivation" implying a deficient relationship between an existing maternal figure and her child.

Childhood Behavior and Behavior Disorders

Behavior Disorders

In this section issues related to risk categories in physical and mental development are discussed. Although child behavior problems are mentioned, the general rubric of childhood behavior is not viewed as a category of risk in itself. Behavior disturbances may be related to physical or mental disorders. They exist, nonetheless, as distinct problems that may reflect inadequacies in environmental and caretaker conditions. There is no general agreement on which behaviors are developmentally important nor on which behaviors constitute significant problems. A brief examination of possible factors related to childhood behaviors is necessary, however, to examine thoroughly the issue of child abuse and neglect. Child behavior and behavior problems are the dependent variables in this discussion.

Many studies of behavior are acknowledged for their rigorous empiricism, while others have been unable to attain that desired standard. Several of the studies under consideration fall into this latter category of childhood behaviors that cannot be operationalized. "Aggression" and "hyperactivity," for example, though considered clinical entities, cannot be operationally defined and must be inferred from observed behavioral patterns. Other categories such as "behavior disturbance" and "delinquency" can be assessed only after lengthy observation, taking into consideration a number of situational factors.

Even though there are studies of behavior that are readily measurable as well as operational, by and large the studies reviewed here are concerned with behavior that cannot be measured readily. They are included because they have been identified as important and, for the most part, deal with clear-cut behavioral patterns.

A number of studies have associated maternal and environmental factors with early childhood behavioral characteristics. In a longitudinal study, Matheny and Brown (1971) examined behavioral differences in twins during the first three years of life based upon differences in birth weight and birth sequence. Through interviews with the mothers of 49 sets of twins, the investigators found that in a group of twins showing intra-set differences of more than 1.5 pounds at birth, ten out of 18 problem-behavior variables were significantly related to birth weight. In twins showing intra-set differences of less than .25 of a pound at birth, only two of the 18 variables were related to birth weight. The lighter twins in the maximal difference group tended to exhibit more problem behaviors (e.g., irritability, temper, feeding, and sleeping problems), and they were relatively less proficient in cognitive behavior (e.g., attention span, vocalization, adaptibility) than were those in the minimal difference group. Birth sequence was not found to be related to birth weight or to behavioral differences.

Battle and Lacey (1972) looked at disturbed behavior in a longitudinal study of motor hyperactivity exhibited by a non-clinical sample of 74 male and female subjects followed from birth to young adulthood. Their results showed that mothers of highly active males were critical, disapproving, unaffectionate, and severe in their punishment. None of these maternal behaviors were associated with high activity levels in females. While indices of social behavior revealed high peer involvement for active children of both sexes, males were rejected and females accepted by other children.

In a study of factors enhancing positively valued behaviors, Pratt (1973) conducted interviews with parents and their nine to 13-year-old children in 510 families to examine the relationship between parental methods of childrearing and the children's personal health care practices. Two distinct approaches to childrearing were identified: the "developmental" approach, which emphasized the substantial use of reasons and information, rewards, and granting of autonomy, and the "disciplinary" approach, which emphasized the use of punishment to enforce specific behavioral conformity and obedience in the child and which made little attempt to develop informed, independent performance by the child. The developmental pattern of childrearing was found to lead to better health care practices by the children than did the disciplinary pattern of childrearing. The report interpreted these results as an expression of the differential effectiveness of the contrasting childrearing approaches in developing children's resources and capacities for coping and taking care of themselves.

A number of reports have been concerned with identifying possible contributing factors to a broad spectrum of childhood behavior disturbances. In a second study on dimensions of early maternal care, Yarrow (1963) examined 96 children who were placed in adoptive homes during infancy. He compared a group of 75 infants who had undergone separation before placement with a group of 21 infants who did not experience a change of mothers during infancy. His results indicated that 86 percent of the infants who had experienced a change of mothers at six months of age, and all of the infants separated at or after seven months, showed evidence of definite behavior disturbance. Yarrow pointed out that maternal care and the loss of a mother-figure have an early and immediate impact on infants.

Effects on children of parental disturbance have been studied in a retrospective study by Yarden and Nevo (1968), who compared the mental health of 175 children of 31 schizophrenic mothers. Each mother had three or more children, with at least one child born before, one child born during, and one child born after the onset of the mother's illness. The results showed that the behavior disorders of the children born during onset tended to be more severe than were the disturbances of children born before or after onset of the illness. The investigators noted that the children born during onset were subjugated to rapid, haphazardly-changing rearing conditions during their infancy, whereas the children born before onset did not suffer from multiple separations during infancy.

Children born after the onset were less exposed to sudden changes in the milieu. Several factors were related to the high incidence of behavior disturbance in all the children of schizophrenic mothers; the investigators cited such intrauterine variables as metabolic disturbances that affect the schizophrenic mother, nutritional deficiencies or sudden weight loss occurring especially in stuporous catatonic or restless states, and effect of various pharmacological treatments on the fetus.

Several investigators have focused on the behavioral effects of institutionalization. In a longitudinal study, Wolkind and Rutter (1973) examined the backgrounds of 513 ten-year-old children who had at one time been "in care" for over a week. Based on psychiatric assessment and interviews with teachers, the investigators identified 172 children as "normal" controls, 241 children as behaviorally disturbed, and 100 children as having psychiatric disorders. Their results showed a strong association between the period of "in care" and childhood behavioral disturbance. The association was more marked for boys and children with psychiatric disorders than it was for girls and children without psychiatric disorders. In another study concerned with the behavioral effects of institutionalization, Yule and Raynes (1972) obtained ratings on standard child behavior rating scales by teachers and houseparents of 776 children residing in two large Group Cottage Homes in London and compared them to the behavior ratings of a matched control group of children who were not "in care." The institutionalized children were significantly more maladjusted than their peers living at home.

Duncan (1971) investigated the attitudes and interactions of 120 parents of 40 delinquent and 20 "normal" adolescent girls by using a revised form of the Stanford Parent Questionnaire and a structured situational interview. The parents of non-delinquent girls displayed higher activity levels, less rejection, higher parental adjustment, use of fewer controls, and higher consistency of feelings than did the parents of delinquent girls. Although the fathers in the non-delinquent families assumed the instrumental, authoritarian roles, within the delinquent families there was a slight tendency toward mother dominance. Interpreting the results in terms of modeling theory, the investigator postulated that a girl, faced with parental displays of conflict and rejection and observing a domineering mother and a non-authoritarian father, is blocked from turning to her parents with her problems. She therefore adopts the modeled behaviors and begins to use the same or worse maladaptive expression and self-control patterns as her parents.

Distinct from those studies that have examined behavior disturbances, there are several reports that have attempted to identify possible factors contributing to childhood aggression. Saxe and Stollack (1971) observed 40 first-grade boys interacting with their mothers in a laboratory playroom. The authors paid particular attention to four categories of childhood behavior: curiosity, pre-social behavior, aggression, and neurotic behavior. Their results indicated that mothers of aggressive boys displayed less positive feelings, were more restrictive, and were less attentive than were the other mothers. The investigators suggested that aggression may be a result and imitation of parent figures who exhibit aggressive, negative attitudes and behaviors and that this behavior is socially reinforced. Lefkowitz, Walder, and Eron (1963) examined the behavioral backgrounds of 875 third-grade children, 555 of their fathers, and 699 of their mothers in an attempt to identify some of the relationships between childhood aggression and identification, and parental use of punishment. Child aggression scores increased with increases in physical punishment, suggesting that punishment enhances rather than inhibits the expression of aggression. Children decreased their confessing behavior with increases in parental use of physical punishment.

In a longitudinal study, McCord, McCord, and Howard (1963) examined the family background of 103 men, 26 of whom had exhibited extreme aggression during adolescence and had adult criminal records (antisocial-aggressives); 25 of the men had been extremely aggressive during adolescence but did not have adult criminal records (socialized-aggressives); and 52 of the men were neither aggressive nor criminal. The results indicated that a large percentage of antisocial-aggressive men came from family backgrounds in which (1) there was almost constant parental conflict; (2) the parents had provided little supervision; (3) they had rejected the boy; and (4) the parents made extreme threats and exercised discipline inconsistently. The greatest direct influence on antisocial aggression seemed to be the nature of the paternal model; fathers who were criminals or alcoholics were more likely to have sons who became antisocial, aggressive men. In contrast to these antisocial, aggressive men, the socialized-aggressive group had less punitive and rejecting backgrounds with fewer or ineffective controls. The same was found to be true for the non-aggressive group.

The broader environmental context of these families was not fully explored, and a number of confounding variables might mitigate the modeling interpretation. For one thing, fathers with criminal records are likely to have been incarcerated and all of the attendant exigencies of incarceration for families would have to be accounted for in assessing the contribution of the parental model alone.

Mental Illness in Children

The identification of mental illness as a category separate from behavior disorder is not entirely justified. We have grouped the studies separately, however, because our populations come from settings that diagnose the mentally ill. Studies of mental illness in children depend on clinical diagnostics rather than on more standardized measures of mental functioning. Analysis is therefore subject to all the pitfalls of diagnostic unreliability also found in analyzing adult mental illness. In this discussion we examine only the issue of manifest mental dysfunction prior to adulthood, as opposed to childhood experiences that are precursors to adult mental illness.

Reports investigating early mental health necessarily have been retrospective in nature because they have depended upon clinical diagnoses and professional judgments obtained from hospital records and files. Even though several have attempted to utilize "control" groups, subjects have usually been matched only on a minimal number of variables, such as age, sex, and SES. Such limitations, while serious, are common to much of the research in the social sciences. They are cause for careful scrutiny and concern, but they do not preclude the investigation of meaningful and relevant issues.

In this discussion of early mental health, the salient topics are difficult to group into categories because few of the syndromes mentioned overlap each other. For this reason, they are presented without an overall organizational scheme.

Zitrin, Ferber, and Cohen (1964) investigated the prenatal and perinatal factors in mental disorders of children by comparing the birth records of 450 children hospitalized for psychiatric disorders with those of a group of matched controls. The comparison between the two groups showed no significant differences in the age of the parents, previous fetal loss by the mother, non-operative complications, or operative complications. Statistically significant differences existed, however, in the children's birth weights. Of the 370 disturbed infants whose birth weights were recorded, 14.1 percent had low birth weight (less than 2,500 gm.), whereas only 7.8 percent of the control infants had low birth weight. Statistical analysis also suggested that low birth weight infants were significantly more likely to have distinct brain damage than were the full term cases. It must be noted that despite the statistical differences between groups, low birth weight was hardly a distinguishing characteristic of either group.

In an investigation of the prenatal and perinatal factors in childhood schizophrenia, Taft and Goldfarb (1964) compared the backgrounds of 29 schizophrenic children, 39 of their siblings, and 34 public school children, all between six and 11 years of age. Their measures were heavily weighted on the side of physical insult. The results showed that the average number of reproductive complications for schizophrenic children was significantly greater than for their siblings and for public school children. Traumas during pregnancy such as small weight gain, emotional shock, alcoholism, illness, and hypertension were significantly more frequent in the histories of the schizophrenics than in either of the other two groups. Such delivery problems as false labor, induced labor, anesthesia, and more than 24 hours between rupture of membranes and delivery were also more frequent in the histories of schizophrenic children. In addition, those children were more often of low birth weight and low gestational age than were the children in either of the other two groups.

In an epidemiological study, Brandon (1970) compared a group of 126 maladjusted children with a control group of 105 "normal" children, using parental interviews, school and hospital records, and individual clinical assessments. Mental disorders and feeding and behavior disturbances were found to be associated with a number of parental factors, including: (1) a high incidence of neurotic disturbance among the mothers (67 percent), (2) many reports by mothers of psychological stress and unhappy childhoods, (3) a poor marital relationship, and (4) an unhappy home atmosphere.

Feeding disturbances were investigated by Di Cagno and Ravetto (1968) in a study of the psycho-physiological disorder of anorexia nervosa. Through clinical examination of 30 children with a history of clearly nonorganic anorexia in the first year of life and an abnormal personality structure that appeared at a later date, they were able to distinguish between two different psycho-athogenetic patterns. The first, an early form, was observed in pre-neurotic and neurotic children and was attributed to a breakdown in communication within the mother-infant dyad in which maternal personality dysfunctions elicited abnormal defensive responses in the child that in turn strengthened the anxiety or depression in the mother. The second form, arising mainly in the second half of the first year, was observed in psychotic children and constituted a form of maladaptive, aggressive protest on the part of the infant toward a non-accepting mother-figure. The authors concluded that maternal-child interaction was an

81

important determinant of this type of feeding disorder.

Three dimensions of childrearing (warmth-coldness, permissiveness-restrictiveness, and punitiveness-nonpunitiveness) were related to the later development of adult psychopathology in a follow-up study by Rousell and Edwards (1971) who administered the MMPI to 64 young adults whose mothers had participated 17 years earlier in an interview study of childrearing. The results indicated significant differences between sexes. A permissive home atmosphere in childhood appeared to be related to neurotic and psychotic disturbances in young female adults, whereas a cold home atmosphere was related to psycho-pathological disorders in young adult males. There tended to be an association for the males between an excessively warm, non-punitive home atmosphere in childhood and the development of strong anxiety psychoses. A cold-punitive home atmosphere in childhood was related to phobic disturbances in the males. A warm-punitive or permissive-punitive home atmosphere in childhood was related to paranoia and neurotic disturbances in young adult females. It can only be assumed that both the permissiveness and punitiveness were of an extreme nature, for otherwise it would be difficult to rear males and females in the same household.

The use of computer clustering to facilitate the process of case comparisons was employed by Jenkins (1966) in an examination of family background variables in the psychiatric syndromes of 500 child guidance cases. Five symptomatic clusters were revealed, each significantly related to sets of background factors. Child anxiety was associated with a history of prolonged, serious illness and with early maternal anxiety. Child hostility was associated with a background characterized by hostile treatment and rejection. Hyperactivity was somewhat related to maternal rejection during infancy, but appeared to be relatively age-limited, since with favorable conditions and close maternal-child interactions it was often outgrown. Jenkins distinguished two types of socially deviant or delinquent behaviors. The hostility, deviance, and vengeance of the "undomesticated" child was significantly related to maternal rejection early in life and to the child's reaction to that rejection. The "socialized delinquent," on the other hand, usually came from a background characterized by poverty, parental neglect, lack of an adequate father-figure, and delinquent associates. Jenkins suggested that, in such a case, the delinquency is typically adaptive and thus represents social pathology rather than psychiatric pathology.

In an attempt to examine the common or dissimilar background variables of adolescent suicide, Jacobs and Teicher (1967) compared the life histories of 50 adolescents who attempted suicide. The group ranged in age from 14 to 18 years, were interviewed within 48 hours of the attempt, and were compared with a group of 32 control adolescents who had not attempted suicide. Particular attention was paid to the possible role of broken homes and of social isolation. The control and study groups did not differ in the incidence of broken homes in their history, but the attempted suicide cases, in comparison with the control group, reported a significantly greater incidence of broken homes or parental loss within the past five years (i.e., since the onset of adolescence). In addition, a sequential process of progressive isolation from meaningful social relationships was found to be common in the immediate backgrounds of those who attempted suicide. The investigators suggested that in such cases a potentially stressful and disruptive event acquires special significance when it occurs, not in isolation, but in a pattern during a particularly stressful time in the life cycle, in this case during the onset of adolescence.

In concluding this review of studies dealing with mental illness in children, the tentativeness of the work must be noted. Most importantly, we must underscore the fact that while statistically significant associations were found in the studies reported, the range in the nature of the variables is very broad. Variables of a differing nature are, however, seldom combined in the same study. Of particular note here is the dichotomy between work dealing with physical functioning of children and that restricted to emotional and affective functioning. We think that this reflects a field where the state of inquiry is substantially at a controversial stage.

REFERENCES

Ainsworth, M. D. "Patterns of attachment behavior shown by the infant in interaction with his mother." Merrill-Palmer Quarterly, 10, 1964, pp. 51-58.

Ainsworth, M. D. and S. M. Bell. "Attachment, exploration and separation: il-
   lustrated by the behavior of one-year-olds in a strange situation."
   Child Development, 41, 1970, pp. 49-67.

Battle, E. S. and B. Lacey. "A context for hyperactivity in children, over
   time." Child Development, 43, 1972, pp. 757-773.

Bell, S. M. and M. D. Ainsworth. "Infant crying and maternal responsiveness."
   Child Development, 43, 1972, pp. 1171-1190.

Bennett, S. "Infant-caretaker interactions." Journal of American Academy of
   Child Psychiatry, 10, 1971, pp. 321-335.

Bernal, J. "Crying during the first ten days of life and maternal responses."
   Developmental Medicine and Child Neurology, 14, 1972, pp. 362-372.

Brandon, S. "An epidemiological study of eating disturbances." Journal of Psychosomatic Research, 14, 1970, pp. 253-257.

Brodie, R. D. and M. R. Winterbottom. "Failure in elementary school boys as a
   function of traumata, secrecy, and derogation." Child Development, 38,
   1967, pp. 701-711.

Buda, F. B., W. B. Rothney, and E. F. Rabe. "Hypotonia and the mother-child
   relationship." American Journal of Diseases of Children, 124, 1972, pp.
   906-907.

Burns, P., L. W. Sander, G. Stechler, and H. Julia. "Distress in feeding.
   Short-term effects of caretaker environment of the first ten days."
   Journal of the American Academy of Child Psychiatry, 11, 1972, pp. 427-
   329.

Caldwell, B. M., L. Hersher, E. Lipton, J. Richmond, G. Stern, E. Eddy, R.
   Drachman, and A. Rothman. "Mother-infant interaction in monomatric and
   polymatric families." American Journal of Orthopsychiatry, 33, 1963,
   pp. 653-664.

Dandes, H. M. and D. Dow. "Relation of intelligence to family size and density."
   Child Development, 40, 1969, pp. 641-645.

Davids, A., R. H. Halden, and G. B. Gray. "Maternal anxiety during pregnancy
   and adequacy of mother and child adjustment eight months following childbirth." Child Development, 34, 1963, pp. 993-1002.

Di Cagno, L. and F. Ravetto. "Anorexia in the first year of life as an expression of changes in the mother-child relationship." Panminerva Medica, 10, 1968, pp. 465-471.

Duncan, P. "Parental attitudes and interactions in delinquency." Child Development, 42, 1971, pp. 1751-1765.

Ferreira, A. J. "Emotional factors in prenatal environment." Journal of Nervous and Mental Disease, 141, 1965, pp. 108-118.

Jacobs, J. and J. D. Teicher. "Broken homes and social isolation in attempted suicides of adolescents." International Journal of Social Psychology, 13, 1967, pp. 139-149.

Jacobs, R. L. "Psychiatric syndromes in children and their relation to family background." American Journal of Orthopsychiatry, 36, 1966, pp. 450-457.

Kogan, K. L. and N. Tyler. "Mother-child interaction in young physically handicapped children." American Journal of Mental Deficiency, 77, 1973, pp. 492-497.

Kogan, K. L. and H. C. Wimberger. "Behavior transactions between disturbed children and their mothers." Psychological Reports, 28, 1971, pp. 395-404.

Korner, A. F. "Individual differences at birth: implications for early experience and later development." American Journal of Orthopsychiatry, 41, 1971, pp. 608-619.

Korner, A. F. and E. B. Thoman. "The relative efficacy of contact and vestibular-proprioceptive stimulation in soothing neonates." Child Development, 43, 1972, pp. 443-453.

Lefkowitz, M. M., L. O. Walder, and L. D. Eron. "Punishment, identification, and aggression." Merrill-Palmer Quarterly, 9, 1963, pp. 159-174.

Lewis, M., B. Bartels, H. Campbell, and S. Goldberg. "Individual differences in attention." American Journal of Diseases of Children, 113, 1967, pp. 461-465.

Lytton, H. "Observation studies of parent-child interaction: a methodological review." Child Development, 42, 1971, pp. 651-684.

Matheny, A. P. and A. M. Brown. "The behavior of twins: effects of birth weight and birth sequence." Child Development, 42, 1971, pp. 251-257.

McCord, J., W. McCord, and A. Howard. "Family interaction as antecedent to the direction of male aggressiveness." Journal of Abnormal Social Psychology, 66, 1963, pp. 239-242.

Morgan, G. and H. N. Ricciuti. "Infants' response to strangers during the first year." in B. M. Foss, ed., Determinants of Infant Behavior, Vol. 4. London: John Wiley and Sons, 1969.

Nisbett, R. E. and S. B. Gurwitz. "Weight, sex, and eating behavior of human newborns." Journal of Comparative and Physiological Psychology, 73, 1970, pp. 245-253.

Ottinger, D. R. and J. E. Simmons. "Behavior of human neonates and prenatal maternal anxiety." Psychological Reports, 14, 1964, pp. 391-394.

Pratt, L. "Child rearing methods and children's health behavior." Journal of Health and Social Behavior, 14, 1973, pp. 61-69.

Provence, S. Personal communication. June 6, 1975, Yale University, New Haven, Connecticut.

Ricciuti, H. N. "Fear and the development of social attachments in the first year of life." in M. Lewis and L. Rosenblum, eds., Origins of Fear. New York: John Wiley and Sons, Inc., 1964.

Rosen, B. C. "Family structure and value transmission." Merrill-Palmer Quarterly, 10, 1964, pp. 59-76.

Rousell, C. H. and C. N. Edwards. "Some developmental antecedents of psychopathology." Journal of Personality, 39, 1971, pp. 362-377.

Rubenstein, J. L. "Maternal attentiveness and subsequent exploratory behavior in the infant." Dissertation Abstracts, 28, 1967, p. 1904.

Saxe, R. M. and G. E. Stollak. "Curiosity and the parent-child relationship." Child Development, 42, 1971, pp. 373-384.

Sears, R. Personal communication. May 31, 1975, Stanford University, Palo Alto, California.

Standley, K., A. B. Soul, S. A. Copans, and M. S. Duchowny. "Local-regional anesthesia during childbirth: effect on newborn behaviors." Science, 1974, pp. 634-635.

Stern, G. G., B. M. Caldwell, L. Hersher, E. L. Lipton, and J. B. Rich. "A factor analytic study of the mother-infant dyad." Child Development, 40, 1969, pp. 163-181.

Taft, L. T. and W. Goldfarb. "Prenatal and perinatal factors in childhood schizophrenia." Developmental Medicine and Child Neurology, 6, 1964, 1964, pp. 32-43.

Tennes, K. H. and E. E. Lampl. "Stranger and separation anxiety in infancy." Journal of Nervous and Mental Disease, 139, 1964, pp. 247-254.

Thoman, E. B., C. R. Barnett, and P. H. Leiderman. "Feeding behaviors of newborn infants as a function of parity of the mother." Child Development, 42, 1971, pp. 1471-1483.

Tulkin, S. R. and B. J. Cohler. "Child rearing attitudes and mother-child interaction in the first year of life." Merrill-Palmer Quarterly, 19, 1973, pp. 95-106.

Van Leewen, K. and J. M. Tuma. "Attachment and exploration: a systematic approach to the study of separation-adaption phenomena in response to nursery school entry." Journal of American Academy of Child Psychiatry, 11, 1972, pp. 314-340.

Waldrop, M. F. and R. Q. Bell. "Effects of family size and density on newborn characteristics." American Journal of Orthopsychiatry, 36, 1966, pp. 544-550.

Waldrop, M. F. and R. Q. Bell. "Relation of preschool dependency behavior to family size and density." Child Development, 35, 1964, pp. 1187-1195.

Walters, J., R. Connor, and M. Zunich. "Interaction of mothers and children from lower-class families." Child Development, 35, 1964, pp. 433-440.

Wolkind, S. and M. Rutter. "Children who have been 'in-care' - an epidemiological study." Journal of Child Psychology and Psychiatry, 14, 1973, pp. 97-105.

Yarden, P. E. and B. F. Nevo. "The differential effect of the schizophrenic mother's stages of illness on her children." British Journal of Psychiatry, 114, 1968, pp. 1089-1096.

Yarden, P. E., D. M. Max, and Z. Eisenbach. "The effect of childbirth on the prognosis of married schizophrenic women." British Journal of Psychiatry, 112, 1966, pp. 491-499.

Yarrow, L. J. "Research in dimensions of early maternal care." Merrill-Palmer Quarterly, 9, 1963, pp. 101-114.

Yule, W. and N. V. Raynes. "Behavioral characteristics of children in residential care in relation to indices of separation." Journal of Child Psychology and Psychiatry, 13, 1972, pp. 249-258.

Zitrin, A., P. Ferber, and D. Cohen. "Pre- and paranatal factors in mental disorders of children." Journal of Nervous and Mental Disease, 139, 1964, pp. 357-361.

CHAPTER 7

CONCLUSIONS

Qualifications in Answering Questions of Harm

Thus, there are definite factors known to be harmful to all children, but they must be qualified. Physical factors in the extreme are the clearest, at least in comparison with more subtle, less obvious manifestations and particularly with reference to children's psychosocial development. It becomes more difficult to answer any question that calls for fine lines of discrimination. Hence, even where the data are more clear-cut such as in the area of nutrition, the threshold between relatively less harmful and not harmful is blurred. Further complicating these fine demarcations is the fact that variables are not linear: too much or too little can be harmful.

The lack of clarity and certainty does not lie merely in the absence of a factual basis on which to answer the question of harm. It also lies in the nature of the question. What is "harmful" to children can only be answered with respect to some questions on the basis of social values. Scientists, including the social and behavioral scientist, can answer with facts about given sets of conditions and about the likelihood that they will lead to particular outcomes. The "harmfulness" of these outcomes, or conversely their desirability, becomes a question of values, not of facts.

Given this state of affairs, we cannot agree with those who would equate neglect, or one kind of neglect, with a discreet syndrome or set of conditions that has been demonstrated to exist by virtue of an already-existing body of knowledge. The persuasiveness of arguments based on clinical observations of children, clinically diagnosed to have been grossly damaged, must be tempered with the understanding that the connection between such damage and impairment of early relationships is yet to be demonstrated.

The direct implication for the arena of child neglect and abuse is that answers for more specific referents cannot readily be translated from existing research in child development. The reason is not that substantial information is unavailable; rather, the reason lies in the lack of fit between the rationale for asking the questions and that underlying the research that has been and is being done. Three principal problems have emerged:

(1) Beyond very gross manifestations, distinctions between harmful and

not harmful call for very fine kinds of discriminations and judgments. In part, information is lacking on which to base such judgments, even in more tangible areas such as nutrition. In nutrition, for instance, considerable knowledge exists about specific nutritional deficiencies, but less is known about total dietary needs or "minimal" requirements. Thus, at the more subtle points in a continuum there is less consensus about both immediate and long-range effects. Research by its very nature is directed toward specific variables and, as long as neglect and abuse are treated as wholistic concepts, there can be no ready application of research findings.

(2) In all areas, but especially in those relating to social and behavioral outcomes in children, demarcation of "harm" rests on societal valuations of the outcomes, not in the research findings. Making these valuations is in fact contrary to the position of the scientist as scientist. As a citizen, the scientist makes these judgments along with other citizens, but confusion of these two roles poses an ethical problem.

(3) For analytical purposes the harm that is done to children can be separated from the source of that harm. The validity of this separation breaks down in some crucial areas in making judgments about "neglect" and "abuse," because the imputation of responsibility becomes a judgmental matter. The division between what parents provide for their children and what is socially provided is a matter of social values and philosophy. In the case of "neglect" and "abuse," a judgment must be made that parents have somehow failed, thereby justifying intervention by society into their lives through allocation of resources to these families and children that otherwise would not be provided. To use Alfred Kahn's terms, services are provided through a "diagnostic door," not on the basis of need, but on the basis of the reason for the need. In one sense, we might say that harm becomes the crucial denominator in resource allocation; if the child is being harmed enough, the society intervenes and provides for the child.

The question of harm is inappropriate for those who have approached the study of children's needs from the opposite point of view, studying their needs for adequate or even optimal development, who have been asking the questions of what enhances children's lives, as with stimulation in cognitive development. This is especially true when work is directed toward answering what is desirable for children that should be socially provided through large-scale social programs. Here, for example, we would point to what we would consider to be a most inappropriate use of such research -- the extrapolation of findings gleaned from programs such as Headstart into definitions of individual parental culpability for less than optimal development of their children.

Support Systems

The issue of whether neglect and abuse are the result of individual psychopathology or the result of sociological variables is a false, invalid dichotomy and pursuit of the answer may well be a fruitless one. The importance of maternal support systems, on the other hand, cannot be underestimated. The term "support systems" covers a wide range, from a symbolic, affective level in total community integration to a very specific, tangible kind of help. The concept of support systems can be useful in understanding the conditions under which the relative absence of such systems can come to constitute conditions under which children might be harmed, neglected, or abused.

As Dr. Stephen Richardson commented:

> The focus on the individual battered child or neglected child has to be broadened to a focus on the constellation of the family. "Family" may be defined in terms of any persons significant to that child. One has to look at the whole patterning of the family. And a very useful general notion to consider for any family is to ask first of all, "What is the nature of the human resources that the adult within that family can call upon? Is this person someone who is totally isolated and has no one to turn to, or do they have a network of social support, in terms of extended family, neighbors, friends?" From this stems a general and rather simple hypothesis, that the head of a family who has no human resources is much more likely to become involved in various crises, problems of care, and upbringing of the child than is one who has a network of supports. We also have to look at the material resources they can call upon because there is an obvious interrelation. A big network of human resources often can contribute economic resources: people can lend money or take the child.
>
> It's reasonable to expect, especially in issues of neglect or battery, that if the parents have no kind of human resources when they get into a crisis situation, it is more likely to be destructive to the child than if they can bring in other resources -- if they can let the kid go next door, if they can get out shopping. A lot of the kinds of problems that we see are the result of isolation -- total psychological isolation, being tied to the child and resenting being tied to the child. And it's part of the breakdown and destruction of the community resulting from people moving to totally new neighborhoods where they know nobody, from a lack of mechanisms of becoming integrated into the community, from a high frequency of physical mobility from one place to another, from trying to avoid debts, and so on.

In these comments we can begin to see how sets of conditions can relate in a complex interaction that ultimately may harm children. These conditions derive from multiple levels of social living, levels over which individuals have varying degrees of control, such as the availability of housing, the strength of family ties, or the use of drugs.

The necessity of adequate support systems for all families, including well-functioning ones, was indicated by another consultant, Dr. Sally Provence, who also delineated some of the pathways by which seemingly simple difficulties can spiral into multiple and complex hazards to children's development in all areas.

> Even two well-functioning parents cannot rear a family of children without some help. In the most mundane, daily, ordinary kinds of things, they are going to need help in keeping the family going. People who are functioning very well often manage to get these services for themselves: baby sitters, household help, child care. We have badly underestimated the many tangible services that relatives and friends supply in addition to psychological supports. But if you see mothers of two or three young children for whom doing the grocery shopping is an almost impossible thing to arrange because they either have to dress all the kids, take them with them, and contend with them in the supermarket or get someone to go with them or have somebody stay with them, then we can come to understand how such a perfectly ordinary task can become a stress if someone is not available to help. It sounds simple-minded in a way, and yet if you multiply that kind of experience by half a dozen times during a day, it gets to be overwhelming after a while. This then can have repercussions on the child through the unpredictability of the parent, who may be loving one minute and angry the next, and the child can't understand because it isn't related to anything that he has seen happen. This kind of unpredictability in parents requires more adaptation from the children, some of whom can more or less manage and some of whom cannot.

Whether it is viewed from the microcosm of mother and child in the supermarket or from the macrocosm of housing shortages and the ensuing social isolation of large numbers of families, the environment of the parent becomes an integral part of complexities that may ultimately harm a child. Thus, it seems feasible to modify the question of "What is harmful" to the more complex one: "Under what conditions are children likely to be harmed?" This leads to our final consideration of the most likely pathways that might lead to a more enlightened position with respect to the management of child abuse and neglect, the conduct of research into the problem, and the potential for establishing successful interventions in protecting children from harm.

Reconceptualizing Conditions Under Which
Children Might Be Harmed

In our introduction we stated that "neglect" and "abuse" are both legal and social work terms. In those fields, they serve the particular function of describing conditions that are a basis for action. As legal terms, they justify the limitations of parents' rights; in social work they provide a basis for allocating resources of social work services and interventions. We have also observed that the underlying rationales for legal and social work provisions do not rest solely, or even primarily, on the nature of the problems themselves nor on the persons affected -- the families, the parents, and/or the children. The very principle of parental rights is rooted in our social and political philosophies; similarly, what we as a society do or do not provide socially, and on what basis, is derived from our social beliefs and values. The barometer of "harm" to children is based upon these beliefs and values and upon our social priorities for children.

Integral to the designation of "harm," "neglect," and "abuse" are the beliefs about what parents should and should not be providing for children; this is a separate issue from what children should or should not be provided, regardless of the provider. The overriding value on individualism in our society strongly undergirds the thinking about abuse and neglect in legal and service allocation decisions. The society does not intervene and does not provide social services, unless it can be demonstrated that parents have failed in some way to make the appropriate provision. Socially and legally, the only consonant thinking about neglect and abuse places the locus of responsibility on parents. This does not necessarily mean culpability, blame, or punishment, but somehow the origins of the failure must lie within the parents or there is no rationale for intervening legally or with social provision. The validity of this approach is as much the province of the social philosopher or the political scientist as it is of the child development specialist.

Thus, our question about what is known to be harmful to children is inappropriate in this context, because if we are to tie it to the rationale for designating "neglect" and "abuse" in these legal and social work terms, we must inextricably tie it to the question "What is harmful to children that is their parents' responsibility?" It is not our purpose here to determine whether this is a proper state of affairs; rather, the point is stressed so much because of the ways in which thinking about neglect and abuse may be unnecessarily distorted and better understanding blocked. In our discussions with diverse experts on children's welfare and development, we elicited many responses pointing to ways whereby these distortions might be avoided and understanding enhanced.

First of all, if the use of the concepts of neglect and abuse can be limited to their legal and social functions, we can eliminate the necessity of expecting that those who abuse or those who neglect are in any way a homogeneous group, in any respect other than having come within the limits of the institutional definitions. While they share this commonality, it should not be expected that they share equally in all or even in most other ways. They are not a separate species from all other parents, nor are they identifiable as a species within themselves or a conglomeration of subspecies. Since there is no diagnosis to distinguish abusive or neglectful parents from other parents, the search for a common etiology may truly obscure the complexity of the situation.

We posed at the outset a model based on our perception of the more prevalent thinking with respect to neglect and abuse. The simplistic nature of that model is apparent in the review of the literature and in the views presented by all of our consultants, who consistently stressed individual differences among children, which must add at least one interactive dimension to that model. Similarly, we have noted the great importance attached to the concept of support systems, which, even if limited to a circumscribed environment of a parent, still adds greatly to the complexity of the interactive forces in the total situation out of which might arise conditions potentially or actually harmful to children. Therefore, if we are to seek commonalities among those designated as abusive or neglectful, if we are to understand and correct the harms to children, we must not pursue the single line of inquiry, "What in the parents makes them do it?" Rather, we should be seeking the commonalities in a much more complex array of interacting conditions, including, but in no way limited to, factors resident in the parents. Current and future research from psychological, biological, and social scientists concerned with children are utilizing that stance from which they are answering their questions.

To suggest that abusive and neglectful families and their children might better be understood by looking at the total constellation of their internal and external environments in no way implies that there will then be ready answers as to how they came to be the way they are and what is to be done with them. In fact, using this kind of approach, everything interacts with everything else, and there is no way of separating out analytically what has greater or lesser importance or what is antecedent. As far as research in the arenas of child abuse and neglect is concerned (and here we mean research where the subjects of study are families that have been identified through the social and legal mechanisms mandated to make that designation), we are a far cry from posing such sharply-focused, etiological questions. There is a paucity of even a remotely substantial body of descriptive research. In fact, until more is known at a descriptive level about the people who are being managed in these systems, it is not valid to draw comparisons with those studies in other settings, thereby utilizing information that may be relevant. As Dr. Stephen Richardson put it:

> Extremely careful description combined with a great deal of insight, in which you work with both inductive and deductive approaches, is really an essential prerequisite for the development of understanding of these sorts of things. For we are talking about matters with levels of complexity that are not amenable to the simpler designs of attitude questionnaires or simple rating scales. These matters cannot possibly be useful without an understanding of the general life conditions involved. The challenge is first to identify the relevant variables. Until we have done that, we cannot sort them into dependent and independent variables.

This observation was not limited to research implications, but included clinical work as well, where it is necessary to determine if a child might be in a harmful or potentially harmful situation and to make a thorough inquiry into a wide array of the child's life conditions and those of the family.

Some of the recent work in the area of malnutrition and children's functional development exemplifies this kind of approach. We do not cite this work to make substantive conclusions, but rather to illustrate that the complexity is not hopeless, although it is not amenable to resolution through simplistic approaches. These different pieces of work are related in that each sought to explain the relationships among malnutrition, physical growth, and functional cognitive development. No simple, straight-forward relationship was found; other contextual variables in the children's lives were found to be more explanatory of cognitive development than nutritional deprivation per se. But these other variables studied, all of which would be relevant to situations of neglect and abuse, are of different orders, and citing any one as antecedent to the other would be misleading. All are important, all are not equally understandable, but in concert a beginning description of important interacting conditions can be obtained.

The conceptualization of these studies is diagrammed below. It is far more complex and comprehensive than the one presented earlier with respect to the etiology of neglect and abuse. We think it is imperative to consider this complexity and comprehensiveness in order to understand more fully neglect and abuse. Using differing indices, various investigations have found important constellations among these variables: maternal education, per capita income, paternal occupation, quality of housing, mother-child interaction, presence of an alternate caretaker, extent of social relationships, child's background history, birth weight of the child, child's extra-familial relationships, social isolation of residence, maternal life history, and maternal resources available. These investigators have concluded cautiously that malnutrition per se is not the sole, nor necessarily the primary, determinant of subsequent development in children. Instead, they have begun to identify a complex of interrelated factors in children's lives and the lives of their families. The work does not tell us why education, why occupation, why an alternate caretaker are important. But until such variables are at least identified as demonstrating such relevance, no one can begin to pursue the question of "why."

With respect to child abuse and neglect, we may have to abandon any notion that we are talking about valid recognizable entities for any purpose other than the functions that the terms serve in social and legal definitions. If we want to understand what is happening to the children, we first must describe what is happening to them. Are they not being fed, are they being bruised, are they being shouted at? If we want to understand the conditions under which they are living, we have to look at a wide array of factors in their lives, their families' lives, and the life in their neighborhood. Although we might not know "why" these conditions and not others elicit harmful behavior toward children, we would at least know what conditions we are trying to explain and into what conditions we are trying to intervene. And we would know more about the children than we do now.

APPENDIX

Schematic Representation of Sample of Variables Mediating
Effects of Malnutrition on Cognitive Development

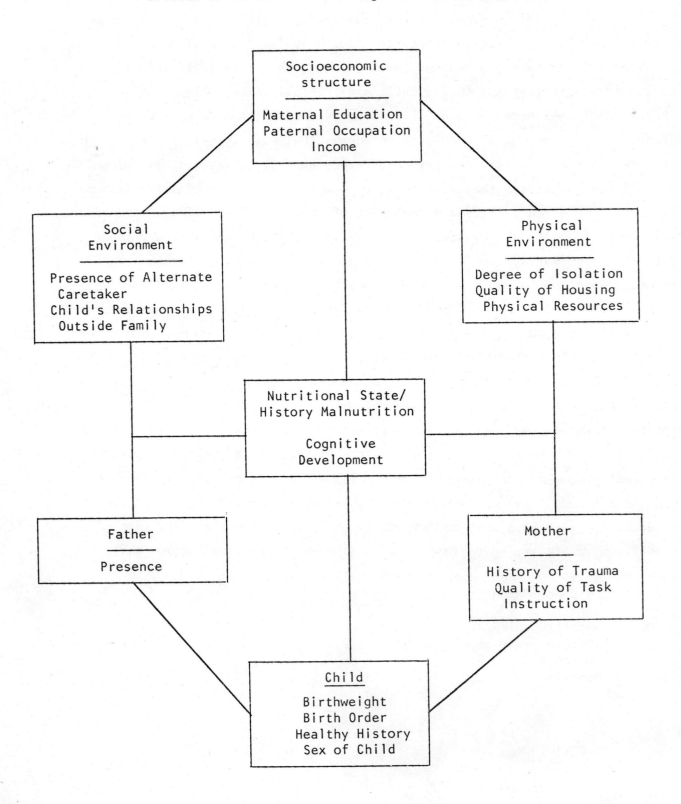

MEDLINE Worksheet

Title: Child Neglect

Pertinent Mesh Headings:

A. Infant, newborn
    Infant
    Child, Preschool
    Child
    Adolescence

B. Maternal behavior
    Maternal deprivation
    Paternal deprivation
    Father-child relations
    Mother-child relations
    Parent-child relations
    Family
    Family characteristics

C. Child welfare
    Child day care centers
    Child, institutionalized
    Child, abandoned
    (Child abuse)
    Foster home care
    Growth
    Growth disorders
    Body height
    Body weight
    Child development
    Language development
    Crying
    Infant nutrition
    Breastfeeding
    Weaning
    Nutrition
    Nutrition requirement
    Lead poisoning
    Diet
    Nutrition disorder
    Thyroid Diseases
  · Thinness
    Obesity

Underachievement
Child rearing
Exploratory behavior
Psychosocial deprivation
Pica

Search Statement:

551.   Family
       Family characteristics
       Father-child relations
       Maternal behavior

552.   Mother-child relations
       Parent-child relations
       Paternal behavior
       Paternal deprivation

553.   1 & 2

554.   3* Adolescence
       3* Child
       3* Child, preschool

555.   3* Infant
       3* Infant, newborn

556.   4 & 5

557.   GK - for
       GK English abstract

558.   TS: neglect
             ignore
             thrive
             negligent

559.   *Child welfare
       *Child abuse
       *Child, institutionalized
       *Child abandoned
       *Child development
       *Child rearing

5510. 7 & 9

5511. Child day care centers
       Foster home care
       Crying
       Language development
       Psychosocial deprivation
       Exploratory behavior
       Underachievement

5512. 7 & 11

5513. Growth
       Growth disorders
       Obesity
       Body weight
       Body height
       Thinness
       Diet
       Pica
       Lead poisoning

Child Abuse

    Child Care
    Child Welfare
    Family Problems
    Hunger
    Parent-Child Relationship
    Social Problems

Child Care

    Child Rearing
    Child Care Workers
    Child Care Centers

Child Care Centers

    Migrant-Child Care Centers
    Foster Homes

Child Development

Childhood

    Early Childhood
    Early Experience

Childhood Needs

Cognitive Development

Cognitive Ability

List of Consultants

ALFIN-SLATER, Roslyn B.   Ph.D.   School of Public Health
University of California,
  Los Angeles
Los Angeles, California 90024

BRONFENBRENNER, Urie   Ph.D.   Department of Human Development
  and Family Studies
Martha Van Rensselaer Hall
Cornell University
Ithaca, New York 14853

BROWN, Roy E.   M.D.   Child Study Center
333 Cedar Street
Yale University
New Haven, Conn. 06510

GEWIRTZ, Jack   Ph.D.   National Institute of Health
Clinical Center - Room B2 A25
Bethesda, Maryland 20014

GROTBERG, Edith   Ph.D.   Office of Child Development
400 Sixth Street, N.W.
Washington D.C. 20001

HARMON, Robert   M.D.   NICHD Social and Behavioral
  Science Branch
4915 Auburn Avenue
Bethesda, Maryland 20014

JELLIFFE, Derrick   Ph.D.
M.D.   School of Public Health
University of California
  Los Angeles
Los Angeles, California 90024

KAGAN, Jerome   Ph.D.   Department of Psychology and
  Social Relations
William James Hall - Room 1510
Harvard University
Cambridge, Mass. 02138

KORNER, Anneliese F.   Ph.D.   Stanford School of Medicine
Department of Psychiatry
  Room TD 104D
Stanford University
Stanford, California 94305

MAAS, Henry   Ph.D.   School of Social Work
University of British Columbia
Vancouver 8, British Columbia
Canada

POLLITT, Ernesto	Ph.D.	Department of Food and Nutrition Science Building 20, Wing A, Room 216 Massachusetts Institute of Technology Boston, Mass. 02139
PROVENCE, Sally	M.D.	Director, Child Development Unit Child Study Center 333 Cedar Street Yale University New Haven, Conn. 06510
RICCUITI, Henry N.	Ph.D.	Department of Human Development and Family Studies Martha Van Rensselaer Hall Cornell University Ithaca, New York 14853
RICHARDSON, Steven A.	Ph.D.	Department of Pediatrics and Community Health Kennedy Center - Room 928 Albert Einstein College of Medicine New York, New York 10461
RICHMOND, Julius B.	M.D.	Director, Judge Baker Guidance Center 295 Longwood Avenue Boston, Mass. 02115
SEARS, Robert R.	Ph.D.	Boys Town Center Stanford University Stanford, California 94305
VALENTINE, Jane	Ph.D.	School of Public Health University of California, Los Angeles Los Angeles, California 90024
YARROW, Leon	Ph.D.	NICHD Social and Behavioral Science Branch 4915 Auburn Avenue Bethesda, Maryland 20014
YARROW, Marion	Ph.D.	National Institute of Health Clinical Center - Room B2 A25 Bethesda, Maryland 20014

INDEX

ACE, 50

Adipose tissue, 33. See also Obesity

Adjective Check list, 49

Adolescents, 31, 33-34, 41, 43, 50, 76, 78, 79, 82

Adoptive homes, 52, 77

Aggression, 27, 29, 60, 62, 64, 76, 79, 81

Alcoholism, 19, 24, 79, 81

Analgesics, 70

Anesthetics, 70, 81

Anorexia nervosa, 25-27, 60, 61, 81

Apgar Scale, 47, 68

Attachment behavior, 26, 51, 59, 66, 71-75. See also Exploration behavior; Separation anxiety

Autistic child, 10

Autopsies, 15, 43-44

Bayley Infant Mental and Motor Scales, 49, 52, 63

Behavior disorders, 59, 75-80

Birth sequence, 69, 70, 76

Birth weight, 14-19, 40-43, 58, 76, 80, 95

Bottle-feeding, 32, 67-69

Brain growth, 40, 43, 44, 47

Brazelton Cambridge Newborn Scales, 42, 70

Breast-feeding, 32, 67-70

Broken homes, 47, 49-51, 83

Caretaker, 8, 11, 30, 42, 51-54, 59-61, 66, 68, 69, 71, 73, 74, 77, 90-91

Catch-up growth after early malnutrition, 23, 24

Cattell Infant Intelligence Scale, 39, 42, 48

Children's perceptions, 12-13

Cognitive development, 7, 17-19, 39-54, 60, 76, 94

Cognitive stimulation, 6, 39-40, 42, 46, 49, 51, 89

Congenital factors, 9-10, 21, 69, 71

Control groups, 16, 18, 23, 25, 42, 44-45, 47, 51, 53, 69, 78, 80-81

Criminals, 79

Critical period for physical development, 22-24, 31-33, 40-41, 43-44, 47, 51

Cultural differences, 12-13

Delinquency, 75, 78, 79

Maternal child-rearing attitudes, 16, 29, 34, 49, 62, 63, 64, 66, 67, 69, 76
Maternal deprivation, 8, 21, 25, 29, 69, 70, 77
Maternal drug addiction, 16, 20
Maternal malnutrition, 14, 16, 19, 45
Maternal psychopathology, 8, 9, 11, 25, 61, 62, 77, 81
Maternal rejection of child, 20, 28, 29, 61, 82
Maternal responsiveness, 70, 73, 77
Maternal stature, 15
Maternal stimulation, 49, 61, 69, 73, 74
Maternal weight gain, 30
Mental illness (in children), 9, 58, 66-67, 80-83
Mental retardation, 6, 18, 19, 41, 42, 48, 51, 66
Monomatric, 66
Mother-child interaction, 10-18, 59-67
Multiple caretakers, 51, 52, 69
Neonatal stress, 19, 47, 69, 70, 77, 81
Newborn behavior, 32, 42, 47, 62, 65, 67-75
Nursery school, 8, 65, 74
Obesity, 31-33, 67, 68
Optimal development, 6, 89
Parental attitudes, 11, 23, 28, 41, 64, 78, 82, 83
Parental marital strife, 24, 29, 34, 82
Parental rights, 5, 7, 93
PARI, 48
Paternal absence, 49-51, 82
Polymatric, 66
Poverty, 19, 20, 21, 82
Prematurity, 14, 19
Prenatal maternal experiences, 48, 63
Protein-calorie deficiency, 14, 22, 44, 47
Psychosocial deprivation, 21, 25, 27, 28. See also Emotional deprivation
Psychosocial dwarfism, 10, 20
Recommended Dietary Allowance, 22
Reversibility of effects of early malnutrition, 23-24, 29, 43, 44, 45
Reversibility of effects of low birth weight, 16-19, 40-43
Schizophrenia (children), 81